# To Eat
*with*
# Grace

*A Selection of Writing about Food
from Orion Magazine*

ORION

Orion Readers are published by *Orion* magazine.
All essays appeared in *Orion* or *Orion* books.

*Orion*
187 Main Street, Great Barrington, Massachusetts 01230
Telephone: 888/909-6568
Fax: 413/528-0676
www.orionmagazine.org

Design by Hans Teensma/Impress

Cover photograph by John Gruen, www.johngruen.com.

ISBN: 978-1-935713-11-1

In Memory of
Peter Sauer

# CONTENTS

# FOREWORD

*To Eat with Grace* opens with an image of dough rising inexorably, "whether we punch it or not." Like the dough that will bake into bread, the poems and essays in these pages expand into something more nourishing than their singular parts. The writers have a way of looking beyond the often hard, gnarled surfaces of the foods we eat to uncover the delectable within—the mellow flesh of tough-skinned winter squash, the sweet heart of the spiny cactus pad. As we contemplate and observe food, it accrues meaning, particularly food we have labored over. No packaged product can yield the sense of revelation that occurs when acorns, painstakingly shucked, leached, dried, and ground, release their nutty flour; or when kneaded dough balloons into airiness under the heat of fire.

It is easy enough to celebrate the overabundance of summer, when zucchini and cucumbers seem to take over the world and the scent of tomatoes fills the air. But the writers in this volume extol something less effortless: the waning days of late fall and the darkness of winter, when a brilliant orange pumpkin can nourish not only through physical sustenance but by conjuring the summer sun. We take for granted the mythical and biblical resonance of pomegranates and honey. But how often do we stop to contemplate, as

Maxine Kumin does, the wondrous parsnips of New England, "those inverted fleshy angels / pried from the black gold / of ancient horse manure"?

The writers here remind us of the earth's seasons, of days both light and dark, and invite us to enter into their rhythms. Jane Hirshfield might momentarily dissemble that "the wheels are only sheep's milk, not ripening souls," but then she makes clear that the cheese maker tends them as he would a child, and "his arms know the weight." The miraculous components of nature, the ingredients of good food, bubble and ferment and rise—this is burgeoning life—but they also mellow and age and decay, yielding a new kind of beauty, and an often-succulent one. As Laurie Kutchins's "Bread Ode" reminds us, food that comes to the table through attentive labor is a kind of sacrament, the smells of a simple loaf "a beatitude." When we eat good food, we smell and taste the earth, and thereby reconnect with it: this is what it means to eat with grace. Gary Paul Nabhan's "communion of neighbors" embraces not only human life but the lives of all plants and animals that surround us, and he revels in our interconnectedness. As Allison Wallace writes, the act of eating itself is "an urge toward union."

Food also manifests desire, within the natural world (the bee's longing for nectar, the vine trailing after the sun) and the human one (our longing for sustenance both physical and spiritual). In "Come, Aristotle," Maxine Kumin invites the philosopher to "come to the table," where the produce of nature's alchemy is displayed. Manure, once meadow grass and straw, becomes black gold; seeds, once mere specks, burgeon into roots that burrow deep into the ground and sprout into leaves, uniting air and earth, delivering connectedness with every bite.

DARRA GOLDSTEIN
Founding Editor
*Gastronomica: The Journal*
*of Food and Culture*

# To Eat
*with*
# Grace

LAURIE KUTCHINS

# BREAD ODE

The dough rises whether we punch it or not.
The yeast is meant for scent.

The salt came first.
The wheat is loving the oven.

The body craves its various breads
as it craves stars in summer
or snow in December.

The smells of bread are a beatitude.
The crusts of bread are undulant land.

Even the baker dreams of kneading
and needing, of smelling and

tasting and salting,
of rising under an awning of rain.

GARY PAUL NABHAN

# COMING HOME TO EAT

SPRING EQUINOX. A day of turning over the earth—churning up dark garden soil buried beneath the winter's leaf litter—to replenish it with sunlight. A day of humus-stained hands and hopeful hearts. Laurie and I pass the daylight hours weeding, tilling, watering, and planting. We work to make a place for vegetables, herbs, and beans in all the unsown garden beds around our desert home. Down on the soiled knees of our jeans, we plant one heirloom seedstock after another, watering them, covering them with netting, and then placing larger meshed frames over them to deter the birds. Once one bed is done, we move to the next, then the next. Even when we return inside the house for a moment to get a drink or to bring out more seeds, we are never far from the musky fragrance of soil bathed in warm sunlight.

This day of toil marks the first phase of a fifteen-month ritual I have begun, one involving my sweetheart Laurie as well as many of my kin and old friends. The ritual extends beyond the planting of vegetables in our backyard. It includes the tending of a small orchard and some terraces of agaves and prickly pears in front; the gathering of desert greens, yucca blossoms, cactus buds, and fruit in the wildlands beyond our fence; the hunting of gamebirds and the capture of other creatures out where the desert wilderness seems boundless. We search for other food producers hidden in our own neighborhood, discovering those who locally grow vegetables, dress out game or can fruits that complement our own. The ritual then moves indoors to the drying rack, chopping block, the hand-cranked grinder, the stove, and the dinner table.

It has no single name. It might be termed "a communion of neighbors." It might be thought of as a "return to the old ways" of subsisting on native resources. As some kind of shorthand to myself, I say I am "coming home to eat." I have initiated an extended communion with my plant and animal neighbors, the native flora and fauna found within 250 miles of my home. The intent: to make me a direct participant, as fully and as frequently as possible, in the making of that which sustains not only my life but the lives surrounding me as well. I want to bear the brunt of what my own eating of the world involves.

Like most everyone I know, I have eaten food of sorts and drunk various beverages all my life, and yet I am like that proverbial fish who has no clear concept of water. At last, it has become painfully evident to me that the kinds of food I eat and who I've shared them with say more or less everything about how I've lived. I realize how deeply, how desperately I need to go home. To go home, farther than I have ever gone home before, to hunt and to hoe, to saw and to sickle, to smoke and cure, to sup, to imbibe and to dine on what is divinely local.

Friends and neighbors are keeping a healthy skepticism about my current project. They ask me over and over again to explain the rule. "Will we have to eat turkey vulture if you

find one rotting on the roadside? Will you remove all the
cactus spines from the prickly pear fruit before you put it
into the salad?"

I try to say something reassuring, but I don't have any
hard and fast rules, only a few tentative hypotheses about
what "eating locally" might ultimately mean. This is no diet,
and it has no defined zones, other than a 250-mile loop
around my home that I drew this morning on an old Arizona
Highways map.

I am inclined to give most of my culinary attention to native plants and animals, those that have adapted to the pathetic-
looking, alkaline earth and the scant, brackish waters of our
desert homeland. I hope to wrest roughly four out of every
five meals from locally grown foodstuff, and I hope that nine
out of every ten kinds of plants and animals I eat over the
coming months will be from species that were native to this
region before the first humans arrived here over ten thousand
years ago. No factory chicken, no pond-grown trout or salmon,
no feedlot anything. But I'm all for free-ranging turkeys and
quail, doves, and maybe even Muscovy ducks. Fish and shell-
fish from the Sea of Cortez, wild "pork" from javelina, maybe
some fat lizards, and a snake or two . . .

Now that I have scared off a few potential dinner guests, I
wander out to what I call the Minstrel Hut, where I do my
writing. Last winter solstice, I had a friend help me make
a roof out of a satellite dish. The dish is perched eight feet
off the ground on a metal ring welded to four upright metal
poles. Beneath its rim, it is surrounded by a circular wall of
living ocotillo branches.

I intended to plant a few squash seeds at the base of the
ocotillo walls. Now another possibility emerges. As the last
day light fades all around me, I toss shovels full of peat, sand,

and compost into the dish, water it thoroughly, then plant
a dozen squash seeds in the moistened soil within the rim.
Over the next fifteen months, squash vines will cascade down
from elevated heights like Rapunzel's hair from her tower.
Satellite dishes into squash planters, I say, an adage for today's
place-makers.

Squashes are native to the Americas, and have been in my
neighborhood a long time—sixteen hundred to two thousand
years, maybe. Their wild relatives, the coyote gourds, grow all
around my yard. My O'odham neighbors, who are the region's
oldest continuous inhabitants of this desert land, love to pick
the tender young squashes for early season eating.

But the squash variety I plant came directly from another
desert valley half way around the world, where my Lebanese
grandfather was born. I grew up referring to this young squash
by the Arabic term *koosa*. When I was four or five years old, I
watched my grandfather as he took a squash in one hand, a
grooved aluminum blade in the other, and cored the unripened
seeds and pith out of the middle. My mother and my aunts
stuffed it with ground lamb, tomatoes, onions, and nutmeg or
cinnamon, and occasionally, pine nuts.

At the time, I did not know a thing about origins. I just
assumed that squashes were part of my family, that is, something familiar that I didn't see much of in my friends' homes.
Whenever we ate Sunday dinner with our Lebanese kin during the tail end of summer, the fragrance of steamed, nutmeg-
laden squash would splay my nostrils. The aroma told me that
my mother and my aunts had fixed something for my grandfather that would make him moan with love and appreciation
for his American daughters, my married-in Irish mother
included. These women knew that the mere sight of platters
piled high with stuffed squash and grape leaves made him
feel reconnected with the valley of his birth.

Today, I will eat the last of last year's squash for dinner, but this winter squash is too big to core as my grandfather once demonstrated to me. I will layer between its steamed slices onions and native spices, then sauté them in sunflower oil. And as I take the first mouthful, I will close my eyes and see if it tastes of home. Because I have farmed squash, studied them, painted them, and even hand-pollinated them, their taste reminds me of a long vine of connections.

During my five-month experiment in local eating, I have often pondered the turn of phrase "homemade taste." The taste of homemade food is not simply the soup your parent made when you were sick as a child, the carrot torte you won at the cake walk in the grade school, or the fresh tortillas sold door to door by the Mexican widow from the next block over. This phrase can be taken in, chewed over, and savored in very different ways.

One of the oldest forms of sustenance in this region is mescal—the pit-roasted heart of the century plant or desert agave, a succulent plant that occurs all around my home. Its fibers have been found in human feces left behind in the caves in the desert borderlands some 8,500 years ago. If local flora was going to compose much of my diet, mescal clearly belonged on the menu.

The week of April Fools, I invited two friends from Cucurpe, Sonora, to show me how to roast mescal. We found big blushing rosettes ready to send up their flower stalks, and trimmed their leaves down to nubbins, using special tools called *coas*. When we were done, the plants looked like giant pineapples, and were ready for roasting.

One of the Sonorans, Chano, who was of Opata Indian descent, guided us through the construction of the *barranco* where the agaves would be roasted. A six-foot-deep hole in the ground that looked like a dry well, its circular walls were formed out of cracked-up slabs of concrete piled into a cylinder. We tossed in three armloads of mesquite wood, let it burn for four hours, then heaved basketball-sized agave heads into this oven, and covered the hole with tin and dirt. We checked the temperature of the barranco every few hours, as we sat around telling stories and making quail traps. Forty hours later, we opened it up to sample the baked mescal.

Shoveling off a six-inch cap of dirt from the mouth of the barranco, we were overwhelmed by a musky fragrance of caramel. The smoky hearts of agave had turned sweet and amber in the process that Beto and Chano called *la tatemada,* "the earthen roasting." We pitch-forked the roasted heads and lifted them out of the barranco. I pulled a few leaf bases off the largest and handed Chano one of them to sample. He ran the leaf fibers through his teeth, skimming the roasted sugars off the fiber, chewing the smoky pulp. Then he closed his eyes silently to compare them with roasted mescal he had tasted at other times in his life, clear back to his childhood.

Chano opened his eyes and smiled, then signaled me with hand jive, "thumbs up." A dozen friends poured in around the agaves and, one by one, tasted mescal for the first time. "It's like baked yams."

"You eat it like sugar cane."

"It's sorta like black-strap molasses."

Although we all ate our fill, we were left with 150 pounds of the mescal to share and savor over the coming months. It was perhaps the first traditional-style tatemada of agaves in the Tucson basin in a half century, renewing a custom that had been practiced here for millennia. The oldest baked good known from the desert borderlands had come home, and had landed in our mouths.

Easter came soon after the mescal roast, and with it an un-
seasonal snow. While driving into town to Laurie's house
one morning, I saw feathers fly up above the truck in front
of me and a split second later the body of a bird on the pave-
ment. When I pulled to the side of the road and walked back,
I found a Gambel's quail, its neck broken, but its body still
intact, bloodless. I arrived at Laurie's door with bird in hand.

She wasn't that surprised. She knew that before the year
was out, she might find a little rattlesnake meat in a fritter.
She'd even begun to express a morbid curiosity about all the
animal innards that might fall upon the cutting board, and
tried to remind me why Yahweh set up a series of food taboos
for Moses and Aaron. I said something about a roadkilled bird
being worth two under the tire, and asked her to keep it in the
refrigerator till dinner time.

That evening, after plucking and gutting the quail, I
stuffed its cavities full of garlic and wild oregano from my garden and basted it in a prickly pear syrup glaze. Laurie made a
salad of wild greens, and we sat down to eat.

We were just cleaning up the dishes when the phone rang.
It was my mother's voice, trembling. I knew that something
had happened to my stepfather, Chuck Buxton, her already-
ailing husband. He had just died at the hospital. As soon as
I could pack my clothes Iwas out the door and on the road to
my mother's home in Glendale, two and a half hours north.

In a moment such as this, I did not think to pack a single
homegrown food to eat over the following days. But once I got
on the road, I realized how desperately I would need a few locally produced foods to fortify me. I picked up a dozen turkey
eggs near the gas station in Abra Valley. I snatched two bags
of Sonoran acorns in a Mexican mini-market at Casa Grande
where I made a bathroom stop. A Pima man sold me a bag of
roasted piñon nuts at a street corner while I was cross ing the

Gila River Indian Reservation. I munched on a few acorns and piñons on the drive up, brooding over the ways I could best help my mother.

After I arrived at my mother's house, we spent several hours talking and making calls to our kin. Later, she dispatched me to do errands. As I picked up the items on her grocery list, I threw into the basket some chiles, damiana tea, prickly pear pads, and tomatillo salsa.

The next morning I stopped by the Farm at South Mountain to say hello to my former student, Diann Peart. Diann gave me fresh flowers as well as a bunch of I'itoi's onions, a desert-adapted, scallionlike shallot. For years, this desert heirloom had been kept alive by just one O'odham lady, Ida Lopez, who lived out in the middle of the Papago Indian Reservation. Twenty years ago, I took a gift of green scallions from her yard, and colleagues at Native Seeds/SEARCH propagated and distributed tens of thousands of them for planting in gardens around southern Arizona. Since that time, their progeny have been nurtured by scores of desert gardeners, including Diann. She was but one of many old friends and former students who offered gifts during the course of the year to honor our mutual interests in local cuisine. I left my brief visit with her replenished by her generosity, and by a box of greens and some freshly cut flowers for my mother

Throughout the four days, despite the need to deal with funeral arrangements and family regroupings in the most urbanized area within the entire Sonoran Desert, I found a way to keep my diet dominated by locally grown foods. While the globalized food economy clearly dominates Phoenix as it does other big cities, an almost-invisible, informal food exchange network can still be found there. Vegetable gardeners hidden in backyards and vacant lots. Medicinal herb and spice peddlers working out of camper-trucks and double-wide trailers.

Street-corner vendors of nuts, fruits, and acorns. Their network goes back a long time, perhaps to the ancient Chichimecans who once traded turkeys, seeds, and macaws back and forth between Mesoamerica and the Desert Southwest.

Much of that old-time way of living and trading has recently died in the desert borderlands. But there is enough of it surviving to remind me of how the world once worked. It is cause for celebration, even during times of loss and grief.

The snows are behind us, and Chuck's ashes have been scattered in the desert. I awoke this morning to realize that I might miss another desert harvest if I don't watch out. I call a number of friends, arranging for four different afternoons of gathering and processing cholla cactus flower buds, a little-known delicacy of my Tohono O'odham neighbors and their Akimel O'odham kin in the Phoenix area. Over the last five hundred years or more, these tribes have shaped a diet out of the flora and fauna of southern Arizona.

Though I have gathered cholla buds off and on for twenty years, this harvest yields new meanings now as part of the 250-mile ritual shared with my neighbors. I learned to pit-roast cholla buds from gracious Akimel O'odham families living along the Gila River just south of Phoenix. Today, I am out with some of the sons, daughters, and granddaughters of those same families.

"Close your eyes," I tell the uninitiated who come out to join us. "Imagine that someone put a delicate vegetable the size of a marble into your mouth." You could not put your finger on it exactly, but its taste reminded you of asparagus tips, artichoke hearts and capers. As I guide them through the cactus patches below my home, the sound of our tongs brushing one thorny cactus branch against another makes a tinny, scraping noise like that of an out-of-tune fiddle.

Earlier I had gotten coals burning in an earthen pit, and prepared an eight-foot-long box lined with window screen for removing the stickers. We pour out bucketsful of cactus bud into the box and use brooms to sweep them across the screen, knocking most of their spines off them. We pick up the de-spined buds with our tongs and refill our buckets with them, pouring half the loads in the roasting pit, and half into big pots of boiling water on the stove. We cook the buds both ways—pit-roasting them as the O'odham have done for centuries, when they lived with scarce water, and boiling them on the stove.

While waiting for the buds to cook, we load my dining room table full of traditional foods the cactus crew has brought along: tepary beans, posole, acorns, piñon nuts, and a wide variety of other foods. Just before everything is out on the table, a quiet Akimel O'odham elder asks if he could offer a blessing in the Pima language. I call everyone into a circle. Suddenly we are all quiet, as this elder whispers a blessing that he has crafted in his heart for us, for the food, and for the land, thanking the Creator, the Earthmaker, for all we have been given.

The smoky taste of the pit-roasted buds is worth the extra effort of cutting wood, preparing a pit, and waiting overnight. They taste of this earth. The spicy bite of mesquite smoke inundates every plant cell of the cholla bud, and every animal cell of the humans who stand around the smoldering roasting pit. I feel some holy sort of spirit rise up around us in the smoke, the wind, the songs we share.

Pit-roasting is an art predating agriculture. Although we typically think of Ice Age hunters roasting freshly killed mammoth meat over the coals of blazing bonfires, it is likely that women and men of the Pleistocene roasted just as many plant foods over those red hot embers.

The caloric cost of eating is not merely the number of calories produced by the fruit, nuts, meats, and roots we eat, nor those we feel as heat while roasting, baking, grilling, or boiling our fare; it is also the effort expended in hunting and gathering, in processing and butchering. Archaeologists estimate that most hunter-gatherers directly consumed a total of some 2,500 to 3,500 calories on the average day, although averages didn't mean much to those who foraged in highly seasonal environments. My friend Peter Vitousek estimates that most Americans require 46,000 calories each day to produce the food they eat. But ecologist Stuart Pimm disagrees. "Way low," he argues. He goes on to explain that that estimate does not at all cover the many ways in which we consume fossil fuels to transport our groceries, supply our gas stoves, power our barbecues, and cool our wine cellars. What Peter and Stuart do agree on is that over 40 percent of the earth's annual productivity is funneled into feeding just one species, our species, undoubtedly at the expense of the myriad other creatures trying to feed themselves on this wayward ark.

After the cholla bud harvesters leave late in the evening, I walk outside, beyond my gate, and peer into the open pit where the cholla buds had been steamed, roasted, and smoked. The branchlets of desert broom in the bottom of the pit are charred, their aromatic oils reduced to a black tar. The heavy trunks of mesquite have been transformed into fluffy, grayish white ash. The ashes and branches of desert broom rustle and stir in the relentless wind. I hear in my head the echo of words said in my presence many times over the last forty years, but now I feel them etched into my muscles as well:

"This is the body that has been given for you. Take and eat it. Do this in memory of me."

Eating is perhaps the most direct way we acknowledge or deny the sacredness of the earth. It has been a year now since I began my modest attempt to focus on the foods of my local landscape, and I have decided that it has been more like an extended meditation than a diet or an experiment. I have brewed and chewed over my relationship to desert soils and salty waters, to ancient traditions and modern trade networks, and to other lives: those of my human, plant, and animal neighbors.

I realize that I will never be a full-time hunter-gatherer and concede that I may never be successful enough as a gardener or farmer to gain all of my food on my own land for a year or more running. I accept that desert farmers and hunter-gatherers suffered unremitting hardships over the centuries. And yet there is another part of my head, heart, and heritage that keeps me from writing off these food traditions as anachronisms, as once marginally useful but now obsolete pursuits. I am glad I have had a chance to hand-pick cholla buds and pit-roast mescal. I can no longer ignore that there are extraordinary flavors to savor, textures to tongue and to crunch between my teeth—wild flavors and textures that I can no longer live without for very long. The wild foods I have stumbled on during these months have been like little saviors for me, reminders that life still goes on all around me, and that more often than not, life tastes good.

As the first year of my "coming home to eat" ritual came to an end, I tried to imagine a way to distill what I had learned and share it with my neighbors. For my indigenous neighbors in the Sonoran Desert especially, what I had been attempting in a personal way may be critical to their survival. These people currently suffer from the highest incidence of adult-onset diabetes in the world, due to diet change away from the fiber rich native foods that sustained them for centuries. Because I had learned that no one can truly eat locally without a support network of friends and neighbors, I wanted to end this first year with an event that would inspire this kind of support among families and communities. I thought of doing a pilgrimage across the region, connecting many of those who live within the 250-mile radius of my neighborhood.

And so this past spring I walked with two dozen friends, of four cultures, from the Sea of Cortez coast to my Abra Valley home. On this "Desert Walk for Heritage, Health and Biodiversity," we ritually shared the flowers, flesh, or fruit of exotic fruits of some twenty-three native plant foods, eight plant medicines and teas, and another eight species of native fauna. While walking 230 miles across the Sonoran Desert over twelve days, we embraced the roadside greens, and rabbits that were abundant in desert fields, and eschewed the genetically engineered corn, the feedlot beef, and the barley-based beers that have dowsed our region in grease, empty calories, and drunkenness. We walked ten hours a day, communed with local villagers, danced and sang in the evenings, but more than anything else, we prayed.

We prayed when we left the ocean, prayed each time we shared food as a community, prayed to help our relatives suffering from diabetes, obesity, arteriosclerosis, alcoholism, and other diseases that afflict those of us with starving souls. We realized how little we really need of those things which superficially fill us up, but really make us hungrier. We found we could do fine without hamburgers, cappuccinos, vinos, and exotic fruits. What tasted best to us were the foods that came to us freshest, the ones that grew from the deepest cultural roots, picked and cleaned and cooked by our neighbors and our very own hands. And then we folded our hands, bowed, or raised our heads to the sky, and prayed together in gratitude for all that lives and grows at our doorsteps. What tasted best to us were the foods that came to us freshest, the ones that grew from the deepest cultural roots, picked and cleaned and cooked by our neighbors and our very own hands. We prayed in O'odham, Seri, Spanish, and English, each of us articulating the feeling of sacredness in a different way.

When we finished our pilgrimage, many people asked us what we felt like now that we had eaten native foods for so long. Did we feel leaner? Cleaner? Did our blood sugar and HDL/LDL levels change?

In response to such questions, the only thing I could initially say was that I felt blessed. Blessed by the prayers and courage of those I walked and ate with, blessed by the prayers of those whose villages and cities we walked through, who offered us support and resolved to do something about their own eating patterns. I felt blessed to live in a region where food traditions still run deep, where enough of the old ways remain to enable their restoration. Sure, our fitness improved, our blood sugar and cholesterol levels probably declined, and we are better for it. But more important than any health statistic was the feeling of gratitude for those around us, and for all the others who are also struggling to come to peace with themselves, their food-ways, and their homelands. If just one more person turns away from fast foods, alcoholism, or binge-eating, if even one more person turns homeward to become a better steward of his or her local food heritage, the blessing will have been passed on to others in a deep and lasting way.

When I arrived at home at last, two weeks of pilgrimage behind me, I walked into the backyard and found that my garden was filled with dozens of vegetables ready for eating. As I knelt between the rows, picking enough vegetables for a salad and a stir-fry, I admitted to myself that I did feel different, bodily, than I had ever felt before. After a year of eating more fresh vegetables and wild potherbs than ever before in my life,

I felt greener inside. That little garden that Laurie and I had renovated last spring had grown in size and in abundance, keeping the taste of fresh green things in our mouths most of the year. And over the course of the walk, I had this preternatural sense that my body was turning green from the inside out, as lambs quarters, wild asparagus, watercress, tomatillos, prickly pear pads, and cholla buds filled my belly and transformed themselves into my own cells. I felt recharged by local chlorophyll. Cell by cell, I was being transformed into the place and the grace I now call home.

KATRINA VANDENBERG

# ON COLD-WEATHER VEGETABLES

GNARLED SWEET POTATOES, tips curling like the feet of witches. Hubbard squashes, big enough to sit on, warty, *blue*. Mushrooms flaring their gills. Back in July, the tomatoes and corn the farmers offered were cheery, Crayola-bright. October is scary: it holds out every child's most despised vegetable in its wrinkled claw.

Cold-weather vegetables are demanding. They require a little muscle behind the knife, and their hard shells can't be sliced as much as hacked at. Inside, their flesh is richly colored and dense. They're messy: *eviscerate* is the word that best describes how we scrape stringy flesh and seeds from a pumpkin to ready it for carving. We wrestle with them. They refuse the ease of the salad bowl and insist on a long roasting.

They are either bitter (Brussels sprouts, kale) or, in the case of the roots, sweeter than the uninitiated might expect. They're acquired tastes, ones I didn't love until I was in my thirties, my husband an even more reluctant convert than I. But this time of year and at this time in our lives, our meals

together are changing. When the air begins to bite with cold
and the smell of decaying leaves, the colors and tastes of what
we eat begin to deepen.

I watch my husband from the kitchen window as he pulls
dead morning glory vines from the trellises. I love him differently than I did the day I married him. In the fifteen years
we have been together, I have helped bury his father, he has
cleaned up my vomit, we have both been bored by stories
we've heard dozens of times. We have lost two pregnancies.
Two falls ago, in one five-week stretch, we were each separately
taken to the emergency room in an ambulance and had to start
thinking about what it would mean to lose the person who has
witnessed so much of our lives. Eventually, surely, one of us will
be left behind.

Andre Dubus describes the meals between married
couples as not mere eating but a "pausing in the march to
perform an act together," a sacrament that says, "I know you
will die; I am sharing food with you; it is all I can do, and it
is everything." My husband and I have eaten together maybe
ten thousand times, in three states, in various rentals and
then our house, at the same oak trestle table. Watching us, you
could chronicle changes — I quit vegetarianism, he learned to
cook, we started to say grace — but the act remains.

Christians regularly take communion, a ritually shared
meal that acknowledges the mysteries of life and death, but
mealtime is especially poignant in the fall, when Mexicans
celebrate the Day of the Dead, and Celts once celebrated Sam-
hain, and ancient Greeks told the story of Persephone disap-
pearing into the underworld — all harvest festivals that con-
nect sharing food with death and gratitude. So we start with
what the earth has given us. We shape it into something else.
Perhaps there are candles. We talk. We have enough and are
together, even though one of us will someday eat here alone.

The vegetables of summer are easy to love, as it is easy to find young men and women beautiful, to promise commitment before it has been tested, to be happy beneath a cloudless sky. I'm still not sure it's natural to prefer what's difficult and unwieldy, to feel affection warts-and-all. But the world is older and slower and more patient than we ever will be. These vegetables keep, and have helped every generation before ours survive long winters. They are part of the great practice of not having what we want, but wanting what we have, and after years of trying—of trying and trying—my husband and I have both come to love, even crave, beets and butternut squash, the hard vegetables of fall. We appreciate their complexity. We find them very good.

MAXINE KUMIN

# COME, ARISTOTLE

On April 4, moving
the pea fence to
another row
we unearth forty
perfect parsnips
that had spent
the coldest winter since
the seventies
*condemned like leeches,*
Aristotle says,
*to suck up whatever*
*sustenance may flow*
*to them wherever*
*they are stuck.*
Abandoned, overlooked.
Our good luck.

We ate them
in groups of fours
braised with a little brown sugar
(though they were sweet
enough without)
paler than cauliflower
or pearls, inverted fleshy angels
pried from the black gold
of ancient horse manure.
Pure, Aristotle.
Come, philosopher.
Come to the table.

TAMARA DEAN

# IN CASE OF
# A FAMINE

*Stalking the wild groundnut*

ONCE I PAID ATTENTION TO IT, the plant appeared everywhere. Its foliage clouded our view of the river. Its vines
tangled with my pumpkins, twisted around goldenrod, jewel-
weed, cow parsnip—in fact, anything with a stalk—and grew
so long and intertwined that it was impossible to tease one
out to find where it sprouted. In August, I was drawn to its
maroon-and-cream-colored flowers, shaped like pea blossoms
and smelling of lilies. I picked a cluster and looked it up in a
wildflower guide.

The plant was *Apios americana*, also known as wild bean,
Indian potato, potato bean, and, most commonly, groundnut (though other plants, including peanuts, are also called
groundnuts). *Apios americana* is a legume, like peas and
beans, and prefers moist soil. Where established, it grows
aggressively, its vines spreading up to ten feet each summer.
Cranberry farmers hours north of my place in Wisconsin
consider "wild bean" a weed and spray it with herbicides. But
a University of Maine agriculture bulletin suggests an alterna-

tive: "One way to remove the tubers would be to eat them, just as Native Americans and the Pilgrims were accustomed to doing."

Indeed, for centuries *Apios americana* was a staple in the diets of many Native Americans, which explains why it grows profusely where they once encamped. Almost every part of the plant is edible—shoots, flowers, the seeds that grow in pods like peas, but, most importantly, the tubers. These tubers (the groundnuts) are swellings that form along a thin rhizome, like beads on a necklace. They can be small as a fingernail or, rarely, large as a melon. And as with other root vegetables, they sweeten after a frost and overwinter well in a cool, damp place, offering sustenance in a time when the land provides little other food. Pilgrims were taught to dig and cook groundnuts by the Wampanoags, and these "Indian potatoes" probably spared the newcomers from starvation. Henry David Thoreau knew and ate the tubers. He wrote in his journal, "In case of a famine, I should soon resort to these roots."

However, neither Thoreau nor the Native Americans nor the Pilgrims could have known how healthy groundnuts are. Like potatoes, they are high in starch. But they're also relatively high in protein, containing up to 17 percent—about three times as much as potatoes. In addition, studies from at least two U.S. universities reveal that groundnuts contain a significant quantity of isoflavones, chemicals linked to a decreased incidence of prostate and breast cancers. Plants for a Future, a British organization that educates the public on "edible, medicinal, and useful plants for a healthier world," ranks *Apios americana* as the fourth-most-important plant in its database of seven thousand.

Much of this I discovered by searching the internet long past midnight on the day I picked the groundnut blossoms. And then I lay awake thinking. How could I not have heard of this wild food? After following my parents through the woods looking for morels and fiddleheads every spring? After childhood summers at nature camp by the oxbow? Of course, I was curious to taste it. My partner, David, and I resolved to dig some of the tubers. But we'd wait until after a frost, when they'd be sweeter.

The next day we visited our friends Erin and Dave Varney, who operate One Sun Farm a few miles from our property. The Varneys practice permaculture, which involves the planting of diverse, perennial, interdependent species appropriate for one's locale. For example, Dave plants strawberries between his hazelnut bushes. Both will coexist happily for years. And he planted the hybridized hazelnuts where he had seen wild hazelnuts grow previously. "I kept cutting these things down, and they kept coming back. Then I thought, 'Wait! Something's telling me to grow hazelnuts here!'" A lanky, energetic young man, Dave speaks with the arm-waving zeal of a southern preacher.

We picked up our dozen eggs and stood talking near the chicken coop in the late afternoon sun. I told Dave about the groundnuts, how we found the plant, researched it, and planned to taste the tubers. He rubbed his chin and looked skyward.

"But no one's cultivated it?" he asked.

"They've tried, but it takes two or three years to produce sizeable tubers, so—"

"It sounds like a permaculture crop! Commercial growers want one season and out. They don't want to wait, to make an investment."

Even after our conversation wandered to other topics, Dave would say, "Oh, now you've got me excited about this groundnut." He'd never seen a plant matching its description on his property, so we promised to bring him some tubers, enough to eat and to plant.

The sun was setting when we arrived home. A deer grazed on the hill across the road, and in front of the deer and nearly as tall, a pair of sandhill cranes pecked and stepped their way through the grass.

I went to the shed and found a spade. "We won't make any judgments," I told David. "We know they'll taste better in a few months, right?"

"Okay, we'll just try them."

High on the riverbank I grabbed some tendrils and followed them to what I thought was an *Apios americana* stem. David dug a football-sized clod of dirt from beneath it, then held up the shovelful for my inspection. Yes! Poking out were two strings of dark-brown groundnuts, looking just like the illustrations I'd seen online. We tugged to separate them from the thatch of grass roots and shook off the dirt. Minutes later we had collected about a dozen, ranging from a half inch to two inches in diameter. A few were soft and woody—the older ones, we guessed. Most were firm as knuckles.

We hadn't brought a bag, so I made a pouch out of the front of my t-shirt to carry them home, where we washed and then examined our harvest in the colander. What to do with them? Depending on the tribe, Native Americans had boiled the tubers, dried them to make a flour, fried them in animal fat, or roasted them with maple syrup. Thoreau also offered hints on their preparation:

*October 12, 1852. I dug some ground nuts with my hands in the railroad sand bank, just at the bottom of the high embankment on the edge of the meadow. These were nearly as large as hen's eggs. I had them roasted and boiled at supper time. The skins came off readily, like a potato's.*

*Roasted they had an agreeable taste, very much like a
common potato, though they were somewhat fibrous in
texture. With my eyes shut I should not have known but
I was eating a somewhat soggy potato. Boiled they were
unexpectedly quite dry, and though in this instance a little
strong, had a more nutty flavor. With a little salt a hungry
man could make a very palatable meal on them.*

But since we'd dug our groundnuts months before their peak,
we decided to cook them in a manner that couldn't fail: fried
in butter and salt.

With paring knives and great patience we peeled every
one of the groundnuts, even the smallest. The ivory flesh,
dense as ginger root and striated with tiny capillaries, left a
starchy residue on our knives. We sliced the naked tubers on
a mandoline, then fried the slices in a cast-iron skillet until
we had a pan full of little brown coins—penny- and nickel-
sized chips. After letting them drain on a paper towel, we
agreed to take our first bites simultaneously, in case they
weren't good after all. But they were good. Delicious, in
fact. A flavor something like a potato, but sweeter, and, as
Thoreau had written, a little nutty.

In the following month I asked everyone I encountered—
friends, relatives, neighbors, foresters, checkout clerks at the
food co-op—if they'd heard of groundnuts, by this or any
other name. I described the plant's habitat, vines, and foliage,
its relation to peas, and its tubers, but no one, not even an
acquaintance who boasts of enduring lengthy survival training
and uses clamshells as utensils, was familiar with it. How had
a once-vital food source become invisible, just another weed?

I contacted Sam Thayer, a wild-edibles expert who lives in
northern Wisconsin. He conducts foraging workshops across

the nation and recently published a book on the subject.
Groundnuts, it turned out, were not only among his favorite
wild foods but also his favorite topic of conversation, though
Sam chooses to call the plant by its Lenape name, hopniss. I
phoned him at lunchtime, and he was munching as he talked.
I imagined him before a large bowl of various shoots, roots,
berries, and leaves that I would be hard-pressed to identify.

"I don't have all the answers, but this is something I can
explain," Sam said when I asked why so few people knew
about the plant.

His theory was that the first Europeans who arrived in
this country found the thought of living like Native Americans
abhorrent. Some foods, like corn, they recognized as "super
important" for survival and adaptable to European cuisine
and methods of cultivation. Those deemed unsuited to the
European lifestyle were not only rejected but stigmatized.
Sam gave as examples from the Great Lakes region acorns,
wild rice, hickory nuts, wapato, also known as arrowhead, and
groundnuts. In the southeastern United States, he said, the
forgotten food is lotus, whose roots he claimed were delicious.
"No European would eat it. Now hardly anyone remembers
that it's edible."

Sam estimated that he eats a hundred pounds of groundnuts a year, in at least two meals per week. He harvests them
in early November before the ground freezes and stores them
in a root cellar. One of his favorite ways to prepare groundnuts is to boil, peel, and cube the tubers, let them dry, then
grind the dried cubes into a meal, which he later reconstitutes
into something that, with some taco seasoning and lime juice,
resembles refried beans. He added, "I also like to make a hot
dish of hopniss, grated wild parsnip, onions, and wild rice.
To be perfect, you should make this with squirrel broth, but if
you don't have that you can use something else."

I mentioned having read that groundnuts were exported to Ireland during the potato famine, and that many centuries earlier, explorers had tried to transplant *Apios americana* to Germany and France, but these attempts at domestication failed.

"I wouldn't say they failed," Sam said. "They just didn't produce within the traditional monoculture model. Hopniss are easy to transplant, but they don't like to be alone. They want to grow under the roots of other things, like elderberry. Or next to Jerusalem artichokes. They're a twin to Jerusalem artichokes. I imagine them fitting into a three-tier system. In Wisconsin, you could have hickory, hackberry, or sugar maple as the overstory, elderberry in the middle, then hopniss below."

It was just as our friend Dave Varney had said: *Apios americana* is a permaculture plant. But Sam wanted to talk about something else.

"I have to tell you, since I've been feeding people hopniss all these years, I've found out some of them will get violently ill after eating it." It had never happened the first time someone tried it, he said, but it could happen the second time or even after many years of eating it. "Maybe you need to build up a certain dose of the protein. Maybe there's more of this allergen in larger tubers. Or it might have to do with the growing conditions." He estimated that as many as 5 percent of *Apios americana* eaters would be made sick at some point and, once they reacted, would become ill with every subsequent bite. "That's the only thorn on this rose. Otherwise, it would be a perfect food."

That weekend David and I had planned a party to celebrate the completion of our straw-bale wood-shop and thank our friends and neighbors who had helped. After raving about groundnuts for a month, I had promised that I'd prepare some. Two grocery sacks full of tubers waited in our cold garage. But on the morning of the party, as I ran about town gathering provisions, I began to have second thoughts. Was it okay to serve the tubers as long as I warned people about the possible effects? What about the children?

Finally, an hour before the party, I dumped the ground-nuts into a sink full of water. I would assume that Sam was right about no one getting sick the first time and that this would be our guests' first taste. As for David and me, we would take our chances.

According to Sam's recommendation, I boiled the tubers a long while to loosen the skins, filling the kitchen with a musty steam. After peeling them, I put the groundnuts in a Crock-Pot with a half stick of butter and about three-quarters of a cup of maple syrup, loaded it in the car, and drove to our straw-bale building. By the time I arrived, I was late for my own party, and in the haste of setting up I simply plugged in the Crock-Pot and forgot about it. Later, a friend reminded me of my promise to serve groundnuts. I scooped out a few and put them on his plate.

"Oh, wow. This is delicious!" he said and quickly held out his plate for another helping.

Others circled around, and soon I had a full-time serving position as people lined up for seconds and thirds. Their groundnut questions became more and more specific, until finally I said, "Want to go get some?"

Friends grabbed shovels and followed me to the riverbank. Some wanted to see the vines, but our first light frost had killed them weeks before, and what remained were nearly invisible, brittle tendrils clinging to the weeds. Yet in our area you needn't follow a vine to the ground to find tubers. The plants grow so densely that sinking a spade anywhere brings up at least a handful.

We and our friends and neighbors and their children huddled in a circle, the evening sun glowing pink on our cheeks and hair, and took turns with the shovels. A mound of freshly upturned dirt prompted outbursts from those who spied the tubers first. "There's some! Here!"

Just as Sam had predicted, the tubers were nestled between the roots of other plants—in this case, Jerusalem artichokes and the finger-shaped rhizomes of cow parsnip. The kids clawed through the dirt to get at the tubers, which we then passed around, inspected, and cooed over. Once the larger groundnuts were snapped off and stowed in a pocket, we watched expectantly as the next shovelful was overturned.

For a moment it seemed crazy to me that everyone had gone straight to collecting food from the riverbank at my suggestion. But of course this is how people learn about foraging. Although there have been a handful of books, and now websites, describing which plants are edible and how to prepare them, foraging remains anchored in oral tradition—staked on a communal shovel, a trailside tutorial. But oral tradition lasts only as long as teachers and listeners keep communicating. Sam had told me about the time he prepared wapato, historically a staple of the Ojibwe diet, and brought it to Ojibwe friends in northern Wisconsin. They loved the starchy tuber, but confessed they'd never heard of it, much less tried it. Eventually one of the older men said, "You know, I think I remember my grandmother making a dish like that when I was a kid." But sometime in the twentieth century his clan forgot about wapato, forgot how it was cooked and how it tasted.

Today most of us have forgotten what our forebears surely knew: that we can find our food in the wild if we need to, that we don't have to rely on those giant tracts of soybean and corn that dominate the rural Midwest. Few of us carry Euell Gibbons's *Stalking the Wild Asparagus* on nature hikes. We seldom look at a prairie or forest and think "lunch." I wondered if, the next time they walked in the woods, members of our digging party would taste-test anything besides the obviously edible wild raspberries—if they'd snap off fresh basswood leaves for a salad or gather wild parsnips for soup.

From five clumps of dirt, our party collected more sizeable groundnuts than we could carry. Luckily, one of the children was wearing cargo pants with side pockets as big as saddlebags. These were soon filled, and the wearer waddled his way back to our shop, where he dumped the groundnuts into a sack.

In the end, no one fell ill, either from the groundnuts served at the party or those they took home.

Given how tasty, nutritious, and prolific groundnuts are, I wasn't surprised to learn that someone had tried to adapt *Apios americana* to modern agricultural practices. Sam told me about Bill Blackmon, a professor who led such an effort at Louisiana State University from 1984 to 1996. Bill, however, chooses to call the plant simply "apios." "It's like a friend once told me," he said when I called him. "'You'd better be careful using some of these Indian names. You don't really know what you're saying.'"

Bill's voice is soft and shaped by a southern accent. He spoke with reverent specificity about germplasms, plant strains, propagation techniques, and about his program. "We had a lot of success," he said. "It took years to domesticate our potato."

His *Apios americana* rivals any Idaho potato plant; the tubers in photos he mailed me are burly and thick on the rhizome, making my foraged versions look puny. When I remarked on the contrast he said, "But that's what we started with."

Bill and his colleagues bred *Apios americana* for larger tubers and more tubers per rhizome. Their most productive strains yielded as many as fifty sizeable tubers and up to eight pounds of edible mass per plant. His group also aimed for greater disease resistance and later attempted to develop a non-twining variety, so that plants needn't be staked or trellised (which requires more labor) and could be cultivated in rows like ordinary potatoes.

Bill's writings in the 1980s, in publications like the *American Journal of Botany and HortScience*, reflect almost giddy enthusiasm for the plant's potential: "We are in search of the golden nugget buried among Mother Nature's tuber cache" and "domestication would be a benefit to mankind." An issue of the "Apios Tribune," a dittoed newsletter published in 1986 out of Bill's LSU department, lists several recipes for groundnuts, including Joan Blackmon's Apios Cornbread, which calls for "1 cup cooked Apios, well mashed." But in the mid-1990s, despite leading phrases such as "the prognosis for developing *A. americana* as a food crop looks outstanding," Bill's apios paper trail came to an end. I asked what happened.

"I left the program in 1996 to take a position closer to my family, in Virginia," he said. However, he left the program vigorous, under the capable oversight of a research partner and a team of committed graduate students. They had been close to landing big grants, they were on the verge of releasing strains to growers, and then, somehow—it seemed unclear even to Bill—support faltered and funding was withdrawn.

"I thought it was going to go on. If I hadn't I wouldn't have left the university."

His last hope had been a grad student who planned to continue to research *Apios americana* at another university, but she decided to study horticulture therapy instead.

"A lot of potential doesn't always equate to realizing something," he said, adding, "I haven't been able to let it go."

When Bill left the program he took approximately forty strains of *Apios americana* with him. He maintains them in his home garden, where they go on producing tubers like the ones he grew at LSU. There, groundnuts were everyday fare for him and his colleagues. Now he eats them only occasionally.

In his twenty years of working with the tubers, he hasn't known them to make anyone ill, but he doesn't deny Sam's claims. "If I were still working with apios, I'd try to figure out why that happens," he said, and then added, "Maybe you could put together some assays . . . it takes someone who'll grit their teeth and stick with it."

Never had I wished so earnestly to be a horticulture postdoc.

Bill offered to send me five or six strains of his domesticated tubers, but warned that they might not yield as abundantly or even survive as far north as Wisconsin, and because of the shorter growing season, they probably wouldn't produce seedpods. He also cautioned me to keep them in a cold place until I could plant them in spring. Naturally, he would appreciate it if I shared my observations.

The following May I cleared a corner of my garden, a fifth of an acre on a bench of fertile land near the river, for domesticated apios. I unpacked Bill's samples, gritty with Virginia sand, from their plastic bags. I sowed them according to his handwritten instructions and watered them well. Then I carefully penned his lab's monikers, like "LA-784" and "LA-7190," on the corresponding stakes. Would these apios take to our clayey soil? Would they produce prolifically enough for meals as well as for sharing with friends and relatives, as the wild groundnuts had? Bill told me he'd envisioned the market for apios beginning with home gardeners who would tell their neighbors, who would tell their neighbors, and so on, eventually creating a demand for apios that would prompt larger market growers to adopt them. Now I was part of the chain.

Bill, however, was not the only one hoping to introduce

groundnuts to a wider public. In 1994, Frieda's, a distributor of specialty produce that boasts of bringing us kiwifruits and sunchokes (aka Jerusalem artichokes), offered groundnuts as part of its Lost Crops of the Americas collection along with appaloosa beans, quinoa, and other historically indigenous staples. "Apios" were sold, washed and unpeeled, in eight-ounce bags. "We had a release party for Lost Crops in San Antonio," Frieda's president Karen Caplan told me, "and we were met with a great big unblinking disinterest." All the Lost Crops products were discontinued after a single season. They simply didn't sell. "Apios came and went," she said. Even a brief mention of apios in a 1994 episode of Food Network's *Iron Chef* didn't boost its popularity.

But that was before the resurgence of farmers' markets, whose number in the United States more than doubled from 1994 to 2004. It's here that America has rediscovered many of its lost foods, including heirloom tomatoes, ramps, and garlic scapes—and, in fact, where Frieda's founder discovered Jerusalem artichokes. Farmers' markets might be the next best thing to foraging. They have in common free taste-tests, a near guarantee of freshness and local origin, and, most important, a relationship with others who know about preparing, growing, or finding food. One slow morning at our local market a neighboring farmer—and a man who'd been part of our riverbank groundnut expedition—taught us how to inoculate oak logs with shiitake mushroom spores and grow them in our backyard. As we lingered beside his pickup bed, he went on to share advice about milling our own lumber and making our own large-scale maple syrup evaporator, and before we left he was urging us to stop by his place and visit. One day, perhaps, we'll have similar conversations over tubs of groundnuts, those gathered from near the river's edge or the larger variety dug from a garden.

Bill's apios did take to our soil. Now, in late summer, beyond
the stalwart rows of edamame and the abandoned pea vine
trellises, one corner of my garden is an unholy mess. I haven't
pulled any of the weeds there, because they are indistinguish-
able from the cultivated plants. Wild *Apios americana* has crept
in and overrun or intermingled with Bill's apios. The wooden
stakes I labeled are buried in pyramids of dark-green foliage so thick that not only the distinctions between plants but
also their names are obscured. This mess is surely a kind of
permaculture crop, one ideally suited to its locale, persistent,
vigorous, and indifferent to human designs. Domesticated
apios vines sprawl yards north through the fence and into the
meadow, where wild groundnuts sprout and climb southward.
In and out of the garden food grows, abundant and available.
It's our choice whether to notice, and dig in.

JONI TEVIS

# ACORN BREAD

THAT FALL, my first October back in South Carolina, we had a bumper crop of acorns. Every day I heard the staccato rain of nuts hitting the roof, and when I walked the campus where I'd just begun teaching, acorns rolled underfoot. I'd read about acorn bread years before, and it seemed like a good time to try baking some, so I gathered nuts in a grocery bag until I had a good two pounds.

Shelling the nuts took all evening, but I found this strangely addictive. There's a trick to it—you pinch off the acorn's round top first, then its pointed end; after snipping through the shell, peel back the shiny brown jacket. When I found worms, I cut them out with a pocketknife. When a taste test proved the nuts were bitter, I boiled them in change after change of water to draw the tannins. I gathered white oak acorns; those from red oaks are more tannic. Squirrels, knowing this, eat white oak acorns out of hand but bury red oak acorns to use later. The soil's moisture leaches out some of the tannins, so the nuts taste sweeter when the squirrels dig them up—if they remember. And if they don't? Another oak seedling unfurls its leaves.

The boiling acorns turned the water dark, and rafts of steam rose from the pot. I roasted them on a pizza pan and ground them into meal with a food processor. Who makes acorn bread nowadays? Manna lying on the ground, free for the taking, but it's a lot of work.

As long as I can remember, acorns have caught my eye. Living pebbles you shine in your palm, tangible promise of new sprouts to come: willow oak streaked with sienna, over-cup big as gobstoppers, water oak packed with sunny yellow meat, burr capped with twisty fringe. Once, as a kid, I made an acorn necklace, carving holes in the seeds and stringing them on yarn. But when the crumbs of meal dropped to the ground, I regretted it. They would never become tall trees.

But I am older now, and calloused. If a tree can bear thousands of acorns in a season, as many do, eating a few pounds won't make much difference. Is this the attitude that wiped out passenger pigeons, once famous for their migration? That name synonymous with "moving about or wandering," flocks so great they dimmed the sun, nests so plentiful they split boughs; eggs dropped like hailstones. My loaf of acorn bread rose high and cracked in the middle; it tasted chewy, a little nutty, wild harvest on a suburban campus.

I think of other oaks I know, like the mighty *Quercus prinus* on nearby Table Rock. The crevices in their thick bark, deep enough for my hand to fit inside, mark their great age, as do their thick boles and tremendous height. They're likely the last few old-growth trees up there, rooted in ground stony and rough; that country used to be chestnut forest before the blight. Now that the chestnuts are gone, you wouldn't know they'd ever lived, but for the space their dying made.

Migrating flocks of passenger pigeons once left mountains of droppings, dark and rich, fertilizing ground that otherwise would have been too poor to support trees. Some of today's mature oak stands may have started with the help of pigeon guano, or the seeds the birds dispersed in the 1870s. It's possible that passenger pigeons gave my ridgeline oaks the boost they needed to survive.

It is good to return to a familiar place and find something sowed with a generous hand. The sun's energy translated into fat and fiber; I husked, baked, ate it for breakfast with smears of butter. What life I gathered and poured into my own. Even though the acorns had just fallen, some of them were sprouting already when I collected them, tap roots poking from the meat's pale skin. Looking for cool damp, and tunneling down to find it.

AIMEE NEZHUKUMATATHIL

# THE PEPPER KINGDOM

Never has the world seen so much rumble
and sail over such a small berry. Dark meteor,

perfect pop of fire—you docked millions
of boats to the southern coast of India,

kept so many folds of pale flesh awake and skittled
at night. Dreams of quicker trade routes, maps

and battle plans inked in case anyone
tried to stop them from bringing back

sackfuls of peppercorn. Every kingdom
must have a king. Let us bow to the flavor

of cannonball and palm husk in our cheeks.
Let that small fire on our tongues combust

just enough that we never forget pepper
first came not from a land of flame and blaze,

but from a quiet shoreline of green.

BARBARA KINGSOLVER

# STALKING THE VEGETANNUAL

*A road map to eating with the seasons*

AN EXTRAORDINARY FEATURE of modern humans is that we seem to think we've broken the shackles of our food chain and walked right out of it. If we don't know beans about beans, that may be fine with us. Asparagus, potatoes, turkey drumsticks— you name it, most of us here in America don't have a clue how the world makes it. Sometimes I think I'm exaggerating the scope of the problem, and then I'll encounter an editor (at a well-known nature magazine) who's nixing the part of my story that refers to pineapples growing from the ground. She insisted they grew on trees. Or, I'll have a conversation like this one:

"What's new on the farm?" asked a friend of mine, a lifelong city dweller and gourmet cook who likes for me to keep her posted by phone. This particular conversation was in early spring, so I told her what was up in the garden: peas, potatoes, spinach.

"Wait a minute," she said. "When you say, 'the potatoes are up,' what do you mean?" She paused, reformulating her question: "What part of a potato comes *up*?"

"Um, the plant part," I said. "The stems and leaves."

"Wow," she said. "I never knew a potato *had* a plant part."

Most people of my grandparents' generation had an intuitive sense of agricultural basics: when various fruits and vegetables come into season, which ones keep through the winter, how to preserve the others. On what day autumn's frost will likely fall on their county, and when to expect the last one in spring. Which crops can be planted before the last frost, and which must wait. What animals and vegetables thrive in one's immediate region and how to live well on those, with little else thrown into the mix beyond a bag of flour, a pinch of salt, and a handful of coffee. Few people of my generation, and approximately none of our children, could answer any of those questions, let alone all of them. This knowledge has largely vanished from our culture.

If potatoes can surprise some part of their audience by growing leaves, it may not have occurred to most people that lettuce has a flower part, too. It does. They all do. Virtually all non-animal foods we eat come from flowering plants. Exceptions are mushrooms, seaweeds, and pine nuts. If other exotic edibles exist that you call food, I salute you.

Flowering plants, known botanically as angiosperms, evolved from ancestors similar to our modern-day conifers. The flower is a handy reproductive organ that came into its own during the Cretaceous era, right around the time when dinosaurs were for whatever reason getting downsized. In the millions of years since then, flowering plants have established themselves as the most conspicuously successful terrestrial lifeforms ever, having moved into every kind of habitat, in infinite variations. Flowering plants are key players in all the world's ecotypes: the deciduous forests, the rainforests, the grasslands. They are the desert cacti and the tundra scrub. They're small and they're large, they fill swamps and tolerate drought, they have settled into most every niche in every kind of place. It only stands to reason that we would eat them.

Flowering plants come in packages as different as an oak tree and a violet, but they all have a basic life history in common. They sprout and leaf out; they bloom and have sex by somehow rubbing one flower's boy stuff against another's girl parts. Since they can't engage in hot pursuit, they lure a third party, such as bees, into the sexual act—or else (depending on species) wait for the wind. From that union comes the blessed event, babies made, in the form of seeds cradled inside some form of fruit. Finally, sooner or later—because after that, what's the point anymore?—they die. Among the plants known as annuals, this life history is accomplished all in a single growing season, commonly starting with spring and ending with frost. The plant waits out the winter in the form of a seed, safely protected from weather, biding its time until conditions are right for starting over again.

Excluding the small fraction of our diet supplied by perennials—our tree fruits, berries, and nuts—we consume annuals. Our vegetal foods may be leaves, buds, fruits, grains, or other seed heads, but each comes to us from some point along this same continuum, the code all annual plants must live by. No variations are allowed. They can't set fruit, for example, before they bloom. As obvious as this may seem, it's easy enough to forget in a supermarket culture where the plant stages constantly present themselves in random order. And that's just the beginning. Biology teachers face kids in classrooms who may not even believe in the metamorphosis of bud to flower to fruit and seed, but rather, in some continuum of pansies becoming petunias becoming chrysanthemums because that's the reality they witness as landscapers come to city parks and surreptitiously yank one flower before it fades from its prime, replacing it with another.

The same disconnection from natural processes may be at the heart of our country's shift away from believing in evolution. In the past, principles of natural selection and change over time made sense to kids who'd watched it all unfold. Whether or not they knew the terminology, farm families understood the processes well enough to imitate them: culling, selecting, and improving their herds and crops. For modern kids who intuitively believe in the spontaneous generation of fruits and vegetables in the produce section, trying to get their minds around the slow speciation of the plant kingdom may be a stretch. The process by which vegetables come into season may appear, in this context, as random as the lottery.

But it isn't. Here's how it goes. First come the leaves: spinach, kale, lettuce, and chard (at my latitude, this occurs in April and May). Then more mature heads of leaves and flower heads: cabbage, romaine, broccoli, and cauliflower (May–June). Then tender young fruit-set: snow peas, baby squash, cucumbers (June), followed by green beans, green peppers, and small tomatoes (July). Then more mature, colorfully ripened fruits: beefsteak tomatoes, eggplants, red and yellow peppers (late July–August). Then the large, hard-shelled fruits with developed seeds inside: cantaloupes, honeydews, watermelons, pumpkins, winter squash (August–September). Last come the root crops, and so ends the produce parade.

To recover an intuitive sense of what will be in season throughout the year, picture an imaginary plant that bears over the course of one growing season all the different vegetable products we can harvest. We'll call it a vegetannual. Picture its life passing before your eyes like a time-lapse film: first, in the cool early spring, shoots poke up out of the ground. Small leaves appear, then bigger leaves. As the plant grows up into the sunshine and the days grow longer, flower buds will appear, followed by small green fruits. Under midsummer's warm sun, the fruits grow larger, riper, and more colorful. As days shorten into the autumn, these mature into hard-shelled fruits with appreciable seeds inside. Finally, as the days grow cool, the vegetannual may hoard the sugars its leaves have made, pulling them down into a storage unit of some kind: a tuber, bulb, or root.

Plainly, all the vegetables we consume don't come from the same plant, but each comes from *a plant*, that's the point—a plant predestined to begin its life in the spring and die in the fall. (A few, like onions and carrots, are attempting to be biennials but we'll ignore that for now.) What we choose to eat from each type of vegetable plant must come in its turn—leaves, buds, flowers, green fruits, ripe fruits, hard fruits—because that is the necessary order of things for an annual plant. For the life of them, they can't do it differently.

Some minor deviations and a bit of overlap are allowed, but in general, picturing an imaginary vegetannual plant is a pretty reliable guide to what will be in season, wherever you live. If you find yourself eating a watermelon in April, you can count back three months and imagine a place warm enough in January for this plant to have launched its destiny. Mexico maybe, or southern California. Chile is also a possibility. If you're inclined to think this way, consider all of the resources it took to transport a finicky fruit the size of a human toddler to your door, from that locale.

Our gardening forebears meant watermelon to be the juicy, barefoot taste of a hot summer's end, just as a pumpkin is the trademark fruit of late October. Most of us accept the latter, and limit our jack-o-lantern activities to the proper botanical season. Waiting for a watermelon is harder. It's tempting to reach for melons, red peppers, tomatoes, and other late-summer delights before the summer even arrives. But it's actually possible to wait, celebrating each season when it comes, not fretting about its being absent at all other times because something else good is at hand.

If many of us would view this style of eating as deprivation, that's only because we've grown accustomed to the botanically outrageous condition of having everything, always; this may be the closest thing we have right now to a distinctive national cuisine. Well-heeled North American epicures are likely to gather around a table where whole continents collide discreetly on a white tablecloth: New Zealand lamb with Italian porcinis, Peruvian asparagus, Mexican lettuce and tomatoes, and a hearty French Bordeaux. The date on the calendar is utterly irrelevant.

I've enjoyed my share of such meals, but I'm beginning at least to notice when I'm consuming the United Nations of edible plants and animals all in one seating (or the WTO is more like it). On a winter's day not long ago I was served a sumptuous meal like this, finished off with a dessert of raspberries. Because they only grow in temperate zones, not the tropics, these would have come from somewhere deep in the Southern Hemisphere. I was amazed that such small, eminently bruisable fruits could survive a zillion-mile trip looking so good (I myself look pretty wrecked after a mere red-eye from California), and I mumbled some reserved awe over that fact.

I think my hostess was amused by my country-mouse naïveté. "This is New York," she assured me. "We can get anything we want, any day of the year."

So it is. And I don't wish to be ungracious, but we get it at a price. Most of that is not measured in money, but in untallied debts that will be paid by our children in the currency of extinctions, economic unravelings, and global climate change. I do know it's impolite to raise such objections at the dinner table. Seven raspberries are not (I'll try to explain someday to my grandkids) the end of the world. I ate them and said "thank you." But I'm continually amazed by the manner in which we're allowed to steal from future generations, while commanding them not to do that to us, and rolling our eyes at anyone who is tediously PC enough to point this out. The conspicuous consumption of limited resources has yet to be accepted widely as a spiritual error, or even bad manners.

It's not that our culture is unacquainted with the idea of food as a spiritually loaded commodity. We're just particular about which spiritual arguments we'll accept as valid for declining certain foods. Generally unacceptable reasons: environmental destruction, energy waste, the poisoning of workers. Acceptable: it's prohibited by a holy text. Set down a platter of country ham in front of a rabbi, an imam, and a Buddhist monk, and you may have just conjured three different visions of damnation. Guests with high blood pressure may add a fourth. Is it such a stretch, then, to make moral choices about food based on the global consequences of its production and transport? In a country where 5 percent of the world's population glugs down a quarter of all the fuel, also belching out that much of the world's pollution, we've apparently made big choices about consumption. They could be up for review.

The business of importing foods across great distances is not, by its nature, a boon to Third World farmers, but it's very good business for oil companies. Transporting a single calorie of a perishable fresh fruit from California to New York takes about eighty-seven calories worth of fuel. That's as efficient as driving from Philadelphia to Annapolis and back in order to walk three miles on a treadmill in a Maryland gym. There may be people who'd do it. Pardon me while I ask someone else to draft my energy budget.

In many social circles it's ordinary for hosts to accommodate vegetarian guests, even if they're carnivores themselves.

Maybe the world would likewise become more hospitable to diners who are queasy about fuel-guzzling foods if that preference had a name. Petrolophobes? Seasonaltarians? Lately I've begun seeing the term "locavores," and I like it: both scientifically and socially descriptive, with just the right hint of *livin' la vida loca*.

Slow Food International has done a good job of putting a smile on this eating style, rather than a pious frown, even while sticking to the quixotic agenda of fighting overcentralized agribusiness. The engaging strategy of the Slowies (their logo is a snail) is to celebrate what we have, standing up for the pleasures that seasonal eating can bring. They have their work cut out for them, as the American brain trust seems mostly blank on that subject. Consider the frustration of the man who wrote in to a syndicated food columnist with this complaint: having studied the new food pyramid brought to us by the U.S. Dietary Guidelines folks (impossible to decipher but bless them, they do keep trying), he had his marching orders for "2 cups of fruit, 2.5 cups of vegetables a day." So he marched down to his grocery and bought (honest to Pete) eighty-three plums, pears, peaches, and apples. Outraged, he reported that virtually the entire lot was rotten, mealy, tasteless, juiceless, or hard as a rock and refusing to ripen.

Given the date of the column, this had occurred in January or February. The gentleman lived in Frostburg, Maryland, where they would still have been deeply involved in a thing called winter. I'm sure he didn't really think tasty, tree-ripened plums, peaches, and apples were hanging outside ripe for the picking in the orchards around . . . um, Frost-burg. Probably he didn't think "orchard" at all—how many of us do, in the same sentence with "fruit"? Our dietary guidelines come to us without a road map.

Concentrating on local foods means thinking of fruit

invariably as the product of an orchard, and a winter squash as the fruit of a late autumn farm. It's a strategy that will keep grocery money in the neighborhood, where it gets recycled into your own school system and local businesses. The green spaces surrounding your town stay green, and farmers who live nearby get to grow more food next year, for you. This also happens to be a win-win strategy for anyone with taste buds. It begins with rethinking a position that is only superficially about deprivation. Citizens of frosty worlds unite, and think about marching past the off-season fruits: you have nothing to lose but your mealy, juiceless, rock-hard and refusing to ripen.

Locally grown is a denomination whose meaning is incorruptible. Sparing the transportation fuel, packaging, and unhealthy additives is a compelling part of the story. But the plot goes beyond that. Local food is a handshake deal in a community gathering place. It involves farmers with first names, who show up at the market week after week. It involves consumers who remember that to be human is to belong to a food chain, wherever and whenever we find ourselves alive. It means remembering the truest of all truths: we are what we eat. Stepping slowly backward out of a fuel-driven industry of highly transported foods will alter more than a person's grocery list. Such small, stepwise changes in personal habits aren't trivial. Ultimately, they will add up to the story of who we were on this planet: what it took to keep us alive, what we left behind.

TAMAR ADLER

# TO EAT
# WITH GRACE

*It will answer many hungers, and its design will be savored slowly.*
—M.F.K. Fisher
Introduction to *Japanese Cooking: A Simple Art*

ON THE MENU that sustains us in 2040, the practical, pleasurable, and ethical will be melded. Those three qualities, which now bang and clash against each other—our squeezing food preparation tightly between other activities, a curiosity in the pleasures of the table, awareness of where our food habits and food system are fragile and even broken—will stop their banging and clashing.

So that when we cook and eat in a way that makes sense in our lives, that "sense" will refer to joy and also responsibility; and pleasure in eating will mean it is affordable and responsible; and responsibility will not be something that complicates the equation, but what keeps the sensible and the sensuous bound.

For this melding to happen, we'll have to start lifting the labels off things. I don't mean just of food itself, too much of which is made by companies that insist on corrupting honest ingredients, then brand the concoctions with meaningless names, like "jungle-berry bars," "barbecue chicken Caesar wraps," and "artisan ciabatta buffalo sliders."

I mean the alleviation of really useless abstractions that are everywhere.

For example, we will have to eat less meat, because the amount of it we eat now, whether raised on rich, fertile pastures or not, won't allow our water and soil to survive. But we will not feel pressure to be all of us vegetarians. With the state of our water sources and topsoil in mind, we will raise fewer animals; with the well-being of our bellies in mind, we will prepare their meat, and dishes around it, in ways that allow us to make the most of it. This will mean a small amount of meat will feed many mouths. Well-raised meat will be made more affordable, not just by necessary agricultural restructuring but by restructuring our culinary perspective.

Wiping our hands of the idea that meat means indulgent eating and vegetables virtuous eating, we will see that any eating can be indulgent, any virtuous, and any fine. Assuming vegetables continue to be what they are—more expensive and harder to come by than jungle-berry so-on, tragically perishable, and most nutritious grown nearby in soil where other animals or vegetables grow too—we will become experts at making the most of whatever vegetables we have at any point, in all senses, whether we are picking from a garden or a grocery store shelf.

We will sagely widen the scope of our larders to include what grows in nearby woods or sides of roads or between sidewalk cracks, and the hardy lamb's-quarters and herbs that we find flourishing on city blocks, combined with the few precious mushrooms that spring up under tall trees after a rain, will round our meals out nicely.

We will eschew recipes that send us chasing after ingredients, and instead cook what is already there, deliberately, in some olive oil or butter, or whatever fat our culinary heritage likes, or even just plain but economical water, with whole cloves of garlic and the right amount of salt.

We will find ourselves cooking several meals at once, and keeping the third of our food we throw away now—not out of piety, but the desire to keep eating well. We will use leftover meat, or vegetable flavored oil or butter, or even improved water the following day. And whether we have done it in one sitting or over a few, our food will have been savored slowly. This process and outlook will apply regardless of season and social stature.

The illusive idea of sustainable food *items* will fade into the far more practical, this-worldly idea of sustainable *ways* about food.

For this to happen, for practices to take the place of purchases, many more of us will need to know how to do simple, useful things: boil and roast, use salt, acid, fat, and heat. Others of us will find we like, in addition to all that, to grow herbs or dry chilies over the stove. We will, in short, learn and wield kitchen skill to make the right decisions easy, and make them taste good.

Because what is practical, pleasurable, and responsible changes each day, so will the details of our meals. Like a boat moored, they will naturally rise and fall with the tides. Here is a version of the graceful bobbing and tilting they will do:

*Monday breakfast:* a slice of yesterday's loaf of hard, dark bread, cut thick, toasted, drizzled with olive oil and honey, lovely if it's from nearby, still good at being thick and sweet if it's from elsewhere; or the last of some garlicky vegetables on the toast, if breakfast is a salty meal for you.

*Monday lunch:* a piece of baked omelet, which took you

ten minutes to make on Saturday, from the last of Friday's boiled potatoes and Thursday's roasted onion; a salad of roasted beets and pickled onions; an apple if it is autumn, little oranges if winter, strawberries if spring; or, regardless of season, a container of plain whole-milk yogurt, drizzled with a little more honey and raisins.

*Monday that awful hungry time between lunch and dinner:* a cup of mint tea, fresh or dried, walnuts, or yogurt with walnuts, or yogurt with peanut butter, and if you are me, probably all three.

*Monday dinner:* Sunday evening's beans, loved equally whether they've come from a trellis or from a can, warmed with bits of bacon and pork shoulder from Friday; topped with a fried egg gotten from the nice people next door, if you live in Berkeley or Brooklyn, or at the nearest farmers' market (of which there will be more, nearer!), where two dozen can be bought at once and kept for a whole month; a bowl of collard greens, sautéed with garlic and chili; a room-temperature salad made of odds and ends and pickled onions; more fresh fruit, or some figs, warmed up in some red wine; and a dollop of ricotta or goat's cheese.

Instead of making a sacrifice of what is good for what is right, or what is expensive for what is cheap, we will just pay attention to how lucky we are to be able to make simple, delicious things from what we have. Then we will be more willing and able to look critically and fluidly at the whole complex quilt of our eating: how we pay our workers, how we raise our food, and how we raise ourselves and each other.

JANE HIRSHFIELD

# SHEEP'S CHEESE

In the cellar, sheep's milk cheeses
soak in cold brine.
Once a week, the man comes to turn them.
Sixty pounds lifted like child after child,
laid back rewrapped
in their cloths on the wooden shelves.
The shelves are nameless, without opinion or varnish.
The wheels are only sheep's milk, not ripening souls.
He sings no lullaby to them. But his arms know the weight.

BARBARA L. BAER

# NO TWO ALIKE

*The strange power of a Soviet-era scientist*
*and his ancient, vanishing fruits*

I WISH I COULD EXPLAIN why I got caught up searching out
Dr. G. M. Levin and his pomegranates.

In the summer of 2001, while driving home on back roads
in northern California, I caught some Russian words on a
public-radio program called *The World*. The segment was being
broadcast from rural Turkmenistan, near Iran's northern border. "The birthplace of the pomegranate was here in the Kopet
Dag Mountains of Central Asia," the speaker said. "And here is
the last place on Earth where wild pomegranates grow."

Sonorous language rose over the sounds of rustling leaves
and cries of birds. I heard the English interviewer exclaim
over sweet wild grapes, pungent arugula, and acres of wild
pomegranates that stretched their canopies along the riverbed.
A Russian-born botanist, Dr. Levin, the lead researcher at an
agricultural research station called Garrygala, said that conditions were going from bad to worse. The station's sprawling
collections of pomegranates, persimmons, pears, apricots,
apples, figs, and native grapes were dying from drought, and
there were no pumps to bring water up from the Sumbar

River. "We often carry water cans to each tree," Levin said. "In the pomegranate forests some miles above our station, sheep and cattle are grazing on wild grasses and destroying the young wild trees."

I felt my throat constrict with thirst as I imagined Levin tending his stricken orchards. In my mind's eye, he had a Trotsky beard and round glinting glasses. I supposed that he knew personally all the 1,117 varieties of living pomegranates he had collected from twenty-seven countries on four continents. Garrygala, the American voice interjected, had been in dire need of financial help since the breakup of the Soviet Union in 1991 when Moscow stopped financing science in its former republics. From the Arctic seas to the Pacific Ocean, Soviet scientists lost labs, facilities, and salaries. To survive, many put their services up for sale. The need to re-employ nuclear specialists was obvious to Western governments, but a pomegranate botanist less so.

Levin confessed that he was losing heart and ready to retire, but he lacked a successor and feared the collection would be lost. The orchards were overgrown with weeds, the Turkmenistan government wasn't protecting the forests or paying workers' salaries, and the facility was quickly becoming a ruin. Only help from the outside world, he said, could save Garrygala.

After the program ended, the fruit still glowed like rubies in my mind. I felt that more than chance had carried his voice from Turkmenistan to my car radio. To my ears, Levin had been delivering a personal plead and an invitation for me to visit the last wild pomegranates.

I tasted a pomegranate early in life and never forgot the mysterious, hard, red globe. The first time my mother showed me how to get to the juicy sweetness within, she wrapped me in a

towel and gave me a spoon to explore it as only a child can—
with fingers, and seeds all over.

She also introduced me to the Greek myth of Persephone.
I saw myself as the dark-haired girl who wandered too far, and
my mother was the powerful Demeter who would never give
up searching for me. My real, beloved mother with her shiny
black hair and sun-browned arms turned every apricot, peach,
and quince she grew into jams and chutneys. The house
smelled of sugar, vinegar, ginger, and cloves transforming
fruit from our orchard.

Pomegranates, each one an ovary packed with seeds,
are the essence of femaleness, fecundity, and beauty. Some
biblical scholars have argued that Eve pulled down the sug-
gestive pomegranate, not an apple, in the Garden of Eden.
Persephone herself became perpetually betrothed to a god she
feared after he convinced her to taste the fruit. Those few se-
ductive seeds doomed her to return each year to Hades' realm
while Earth suffered its winter death.

In the spring, Persephone returns to Earth, just as the
pomegranate trees begin to leaf out. Soon the fragrant scarlet
or peach or white blossoms open on branch tips. After bees
pollinate the blossoms, flesh-wrapped seeds begin to grow
around each original flower. As the abundant treasures expand within the tough outer skin, the six-petaled calyx contin-
ues to hang down, revealing the fruit's plump sexual parts, as
if the seduction were never over. In late fall, when most other
fruit trees stand with bare branches, many varieties of pomegranates blossom again and again, their amphora-shaped petals swishing on new wood like Persephone's skirts.

I knew from experience that fall was the best time to visit
Central Asia. For two years in the late 1960s I'd lived in
Uzbekistan, teaching English at the University of Tashkent.

The radio program drew me back to my first autumn there, to bazaars so perfumed with ripe fruit that bees fell into the red flesh of opened pomegranates and figs. With Levin's voice still echoing in my head, I grew determined to visit Garrygala and the wild pomegranate forests.

A month after the radio program, September 11 happened, and obtaining visas to Central Asia became exceedingly difficult. Nonetheless, I began applying for permission to enter Turkmenistan even as American troops were setting up bases there to fight the war in neighboring Afghanistan. At the same time I tried to get in touch with Levin at Garrygala, but there was no internet connection at the research station. I relied on Dr. Muhabbat Turdieva, a plant geneticist at Tashkent University, to keep me apprised of the situation in Turkmenistan while I waited for my visa.

For a year, she sent me news of Levin and forwarded his articles, translated into awkward English. From her I learned that Levin had arrived at the Garrygala Agricultural Station in the 1950s and found high mountains that provided fruit trees with a perfect barrier against cold winters and hot desert summers. There was also dependable rainfall, and a frost-free period of more than two hundred days. Using Garrygala as his base, Levin had spent most of his adult life trekking around Central Asia and the Caucasus in search of pomegranates, writing more than 150 scientific papers on the topic, and tending the orchards at the station.

By poring over everything from Levin's papers to articles in *Agricultural Research*, I absorbed a trove of information. I also began simplifying Levin's scientific prose into something readable for a fundraising brochure for the research station.

I knew I would have to leave out the more specialized but fascinating information about the pomegranate, an aggregate fruit that develops hundreds of individual "fruitlets," or juicy arils, within its leathery skin. And despite my notion of pome-granates tennis ball–sized globes, I learned of dryish, fig-sized Yemenite varieties and Persian pomegranates called Saveh that are big as a baby's head, with purple skin and super-sweet arils. While cultivated pomegranate trees can bear one hun-dred pounds of fruit a year, their bushier wild progenitors grow in groups of up to a thousand with canopies stretching thirty feet high.

By studying the pomegranate on my own, I traced its path into antiquity. The fruit's botanical name, *Punica granatum*, came by way of ancient Carthage, which the Romans knew as Punica, and where they encountered the fruit for the first time. Farther to the east and still further back into antiquity, Moses' priests are said to have worn pomegranate-embossed robes. The pillars of Solomon's Temple were decorated with them. In the Koran, as in Persian iconography and poetry, images of pomegranates symbolized fertility, and in China, a bride and groom went to bed with seeds scattered on their covers to assure conception.

The pomegranate was well known too on the medieval Silk Road where traders and Bedouins relied on its soothing juice while crossing the steppes of Kazakhstan, the Kara Kum and Kizilkum deserts of Central Asia, the blowing sands of Arabia, and the Gobi expanses of Mongolia and China.

In the early sixteenth century, the Spanish carried crate-loads of them across the sea because the vitamin C–rich fruit, protected by its leatherlike casing, guarded sailors against scurvy. The friars on board, meanwhile, brought roots to plant in the New World, where the fruit flourishes four hundred years later in California's Mediterranean climate.

Folk healers have long used every part of the fruit to staunch wounds and treat illnesses like dyspepsia and leprosy. Powdered flower buds helped clear the lungs. Bark, leaves, and rind served as astringents to treat diarrhea, dysentery, and tapeworm. A friend of mine in Tashkent remembers having to drink a bitter brew made from soaked pomegranate rind every time she had a childhood stomachache.

These days, scientists in Israel have been actively researching the fruit's pharmaceutical properties (the country harvests three thousand tons annually) to battle everything from viruses to breast cancer and aging skin. The pomegranate contains a flavonoid that is a powerful cancer-fighting antioxidant. The fruit is also rich in estrogen, and one company is now marketing pomegranate-derived EstraGranate as an alternative to hormone-replacement therapy. In the works is a condom coated with pomegranate juice that will reportedly fend off HIV.

In rural Sonoma County, California, where I live, stores now carry pomegranates from fall through winter, thanks to one of America's biggest corporate growers, Paramount Farms.

They market a single variety, Wonderful, that is grown on six thousand acres in California's Central Valley. In the midst of my own pomegranate thrall, Paramount's juice drink, Pom Wonderful, began appearing in specialty stores along with recipes for cooking with the new fruit. I tried out Middle Eastern stews and created gorgeous salads topped with big red Wonderful seeds, but when I wanted to expand to other varieties, I struck out. Every inquiry in food markets and nurseries resulted in the same answer; sorry, we only have Wonderful.

Because I talked obsessively about the fruit, friends found prints and postcards for my study. A visitor to London sent my favorite image, a reproduction of an eighteenth-century French silk tapestry from the Victoria and Albert Museum showing a gnarled bough loaded with giant red globes hanging over castle turrets and stairs half submerged in a turbulent sea. Last year, I couldn't resist buying a dramatic three-foot-by-two-foot monotype print by Massachusetts artist Celia Gilbert—red pomegranate on a black background, with a quarter-dissection showing bundles of seeds that look like messages in a bottle.

Early in 2002, I sent $500 to Muhabbat to print the fund-raising brochure we had created together. I hoped that *Ruby Treasure: Securing the Wealth of Pomegranates in Central Asia* might reach donors who would help finance the rescue of Turkmenistan's wild pomegranates and the station's irreplaceable collection. The brochure felt like my own passport to Garrygala—but still I waited for my visa to arrive.

In Turkmenistan, where Levin had collected his 1,117 different rare and unusual varieties, the news was not good: both wild forests and trees in Garrygala's collection—"the unique wild and cultivated patrimony," as Levin had written in one scientific paper—were dying. The irony, of course, was that as Wonderful was being pumped up and juiced out, the original pomegranates—those that might one day be needed to save a monoculture afflicted with pests and disease—were withering away.

When my tourist visa finally arrived, I was granted a week in Turkmenistan with a tour group leaving that October. I had hoped to travel alone, but a tour proved the only way to get in. Muhabbat assured me there would be time to go with her to Garrygala while my group visited the capital, Ashgabat.

We flew from Istanbul to Tashkent, and then went by bus to Ashgabat. The first image that greeted us on the Turkmenistan side of the Amu Darya was the huge billboard-sized head and small squinty eyes of Turkmenbashi, the country's all-seeing, all-powerful dictator. Whenever a village appeared, so did the dictator's visage, and his little eyes seemed to follow us from above.

Saparmurat Niyazov, Turkmen Communist Party chair-
man when the Soviet Union collapsed, took power in 1991
and soon renamed himself Turkmenbashi the Great, Father-
Leader Greatest of All Turkmen. In 1999, a rubber-stamp leg-
islature elected him president for life, and in the decade since,
he has dedicated the resources of his impoverished country
to a Stalinesque personality cult, renaming cities, streets,
mosques, factories, airports, and even days of the week after
himself. And lest one forget him in the privacy of the home,
his face appears on postage stamps, vodka bottles, teabags,
and in digitally enhanced images on every TV screen.

"You are fortunate to be in Turkmenistan in October," Ali,
our guide, told me, "because October—actually we no longer
call it October but Rukhnama—is the most important month
of the year. It is the anniversary of the terrible earthquake, of
our Independence Day, and the month our president published *Rukhnama*."

Variously translated as *Soul of the People* or *Spiritual Re-
newal*, *Rukhnama* is Turkmenbashi's little red book—red but
not so little. It's meant to be recited every Saturday along with
the Koran, and in it Turkmenbashi instructs Turkmen on the
correct ways to live. No detail is neglected. Nor are his poetry,
religious maxims, or handwriting—reproductions of which
are included. As Ali continued praising the powers of this
book (the traditional Islamic greeting had been amended to
*Asalemaleikim rukhnama*), I began to have a bad feeling about
October/Rukhnama, remembering similar Soviet propaganda-
laden holidays that brought life to a halt.

Out of the desert blackness our bus approached Ashgabat,
which glowed with a million lights. Massive pillared structures,
inspired by the Greeks, Romans, and Persians, stood eerily
illuminated on broad, empty avenues. Trevi-like fountains
spouted plumes of colored water. At the highest point, visible

for miles around, the golden statue of Turkmenbashi rotated 220 feet in the air.

"He always turns to the sun," said Ali, who used to teach English in a village school until Turkmenbashi eliminated foreign languages from the national curriculum. I remarked that the sun wasn't out. "He doesn't rest, not even at night," replied Ali. Wizard of Oz, I thought. Ozymandias.

The next morning I looked out the window of my Ashgabat hotel room through a hazy sky to the Kopet Dag range, which runs southeast along Turkmenistan's border with Iran and peters out near Afghanistan. The tan ridges, dangerous old crags on a major tectonic fault line, appeared deceptively soft through smog. Six stories below, hundreds of pigeons were using an Olympic-sized pool for a bath.

By the time my group left on a city tour, Muhabbat still hadn't registered. I waited in the lobby, worrying over our last e-mails, in which she'd written of difficulties obtaining a visa to travel from Uzbekistan. Two modestly dressed people stepped through the revolving doors. One was a stocky woman with flat Central Asian features, dressed severely in a Soviet-era black suit that matched her grim expression. I hoped she wasn't Muhabbat. Beside her stood an elegant, slender man in his fifties who looked like a Chinese sage.

"Miss Barbara?" asked the woman. "I am Dr. Lena, a native plant specialist at Ashgabat University. Thank you for your interest in us. Dr. G. M. Levin has recently emigrated to Israel. I would like to present the director of Garrygala Experimental Station, Dr. Makmud Isar." Isar, she said, had taken a bus from Garrygala at four in the morning to be here.

"We are preparing for Independence Day," Lena said. "Because Garrygala is located close to the border with Iran, for security reasons the authorities have decided it is too dangerous for you to travel there." She avoided my eyes.

"In three days, I'll be crossing into Iran myself," I said, realizing that my dream of visiting Garrygala was vanishing before my eyes. "The holiday is two weeks away."

"Dr. Muhabbat Turdieva also failed to get a visa from Tashkent," Lena said, handing me two heavy books praising the environmental work of Turkmenbashi. She was flying on to China that day for a conference, but Dr. Isar had come to show me the city. He shyly presented me with two huge paper sacks of pomegranates and said in Russian, "We are so sorry for the trouble," looking truly embarrassed.

The pomegranates were nestled like Christmas balls in tissue; garnet, cream-colored, and hot-pink tokens to make up for not seeing them in their natural glory.

Isar invited me to take a walk, and so, feeling shocked, I ambled beside him. The sun glared off glass and metal facades. Cars spewed black exhaust. Smog now completely blurred the Kopet Dag's eleven-thousand-foot escarpment. Inexplicably, the part of my brain that remembered the Russian I spoke thirty years ago kicked in, and I found myself understanding most of Isar's softly uttered comments.

He said that Turkmenbashi gave every citizen free water, electricity, and gas, but cars were old and new parts unavailable, thus the pollution problem. Since the president had given up cigarettes, he'd forbidden smoking in public. According to recent decrees, radios must not be played in public. Young men must cut long hair and shave their beards.

We stood before a massive fountain where marble steeds pawed the hot air over cascading waterfalls. Isar said it was the biggest fountain in the world. What I saw was not a wonder of Rome but an aquatic extravagance in the desert. At Garrygala the trees were dying of thirst. Isar said only, "If we had a mini tractor, we could dig deeper wells to bring water from the Sumbar River." It isn't just Garrygala that suffers in Turkmenistan. Despite massive infusions of dollars for rights to natural gas and oil paid by U.S. and international corporations, the national bank is insolvent, university degrees are no longer accredited abroad, official unemployment is listed at 25 percent but is more likely 50, and most recently, the school year has been shortened to stem budget deficits. How many gold statues and domes, marble-pillared halls and fountains did it take to run a budget deficit with so much oil and gas?

We approached the pseudo–Eiffel Tower atop which a thirty-six-foot-tall golden statue of Turkmenbashi slowly rotated.

"He always turns facing the sun," Isar said flatly.

We rode an exterior glass elevator up the tower. Around us, a crowd of shabbily dressed people pressed their noses to the glass, open-mouthed and wide-eyed. To these peasants, perhaps, Turkmenbashi had built wonders. To them he was a golden man, a khan of old, a prophet who protected them with his raised gilded arm.

"My daughters will prepare you Turkmen pilaf," Isar said later as we walked in the tower's shadow. He hailed a taxi, greeting the driver, who was a school friend. I watched the glass-and-concrete no-man's-land of government palaces give way to older apartments, then tenement walls and tilting wooden houses where laundry flapped on balconies in the desert wind. We drove up a potholed alley to a poor neighborhood only ten minutes from Turkmenbashi's glittering monuments, where Isar kept his house open for his two sons, who studied at the university.

His daughters lived with their husbands in Ashgabat but came at their father's call to cook a traditional meal. As the lamb sizzled in fat on a two-burner stove, Isar and his sons began to roll pomegranates out on a flowered quilt. They were yellow, pink, peach, crimson, maroon, and purple—no two alike. Isar expertly opened one after another. Some had an acidic bite, others were boldly sweet, and a big pink one tasted like honey. As I swallowed the seeds, my eyes filled with tears. This was not Garrygala I'd reached, but I felt such sympathy for Isar and so welcomed by him that I could almost believe the trees stood before me in his living room.

"My pomegranate wine," Isar said, uncorking two murky bottles. "Good for digestion." The wine tasted medicinal yet sweet, like *genepi*, the herb wine of Provence.

After dinner, Isar lugged the pomegranates into a taxi and we drove back to Ashgabat's center. The night was warm, the imperial fountains cool. We wandered from one to another, sometimes talking, sometimes silent, reluctant to say good night. Arriving finally at the hotel, I thanked him. "For every-thing, the pomegranates especially," I said.

The morning Grigory Levin's name popped up on e-mail, I was too moved to open it immediately—it was the first time I'd even seen his first name. "Dear Madam Barbara I thank you for your letter," wrote Levin, who used a web-based trans-lation software to turn Russian into English. "It was very pleasant to me to found out that in U.S.A. there are still peo-ple whom pomegranate interests."

Nearly two years had passed since I had gone in search of Levin and his pomegranates, and I remained unable to forget the sound of the Russian botanist's voice coming over my car radio. I had stayed in touch with Muhabbat, who had sent news that Isar had been promoted to a job at the agricultural ministry, where he had secured a small sum to pay for irrigat-ing pumps at Garrygala. Some staff had received salaries, and conditions had slightly improved. The Global Crop Diversity Trust that supports apple collections had indicated that it might give the pomegranates some help. Still, old machinery needed repair and the water problem was far from resolved.

Had she heard anything of Levin, I had asked. Wanting to know why he left and what had happened to his research, I began searching for him—with no luck until a dedicated woman in the Agriculture Section of the Israeli Embassy in Washington treated my request as if it were a family matter and hunted through all the Levins in Israel for a pomegranate specialist.

Levin in his e-mail wrote that he'd left Garrygala as the station started to break up before his eyes. The collection he'd tended for years was perishing, and that had become too painful to watch. He'd brought plantings to Israel where the pomegranates were growing well and now he wanted his life's work—what he called a theoretical book on pomegranates—to reach a larger audience. He wished that his "work done has not gone to waste and was accessible to science. This is our common cause."

Once again I began dreaming about, and planning on, helping Grigory Levin. On a brilliant November day last year, I visited the Wolfskill Experimental Orchard at the University of California at Davis—also known as one of several National Clonal Germplasm Repositories. The official title was made informal by two enthusiastic young men—greenhouse manager Jeff Moersfelder and his technical assistant Joe Wehrheim—who spent their afternoon with me. As we slipped around in thick soil made mud by the fall's first rains, they cracked open red, purple, and yellow pomegranate globes for me to taste. Hanging alongside mature fruit, color-coordinated flowers glowed against the blue sky. The extended flowering time, Moersfelder explained, happened only in experimental orchards like Wolfskill, or Garrygala, where numerous varieties grew together in what he called "a tree museum." In a commercial orchard such as Paramount Farms, by contrast, timing is not left to nature. There, all the cloned Wonderful

pomegranate trees would bloom at the same time and produce fruit conveniently on schedule for workers to pick. Then
Moersfelder showed me trees marked PROVENANCE TURKMEN-
ISTAN. It was as if I knew them. *Parfyanka* was big and pinkish
rose, with soft seeds. *Azadi* was peach-colored and delicate as
a flower. *Girkanski* was dark, almost purple, with a wine-rich
flavor. Moersfelder probed the arils to show me seeds, some
large and soft, others hard and small.

I asked where, exactly, had the trees come from? "Central
Asia," Moersfelder answered. "I wish we knew more about
their origin and biological history."

"They must have come from Grigory Levin," I said. "He
managed the largest collection of pomegranates in the world
in Turkmenistan."

Moersfelder and Wehrheim, grape specialists by training
who also had been seduced by the pomegranate, grew excited
about tracking down the biological roots of their trees. Next
time I came, they urged, I'd have to try their pomegranate
wine. I told them about drinking Isar's wine and how to reach
Levin in Israel. Days later, Grigory wrote that the UC Davis
botanists had contacted him. Indeed, he knew their pomegranates well. "Of course," he wrote. "I personally sent them
pomegranates."

I suggested to him that his adventures as a pomegranate
explorer and his descriptions of forays in the Transcaucasus
and Central Asia could make for a fine book for my small
publishing house, Floreant Press. I envisioned pomegranate
paintings and photographs from Turkmenistan and California. Levin responded immediately: "Forty years I am engaged
as hunter behind plants, gathering and creating collection. I
am calmed by this news and hope that work is not vain, but
also sometime will be read. For this, my gratitude does not
have borders."

For the past half year, Grigory has been recalling his pomegranate adventures for the book I plan to publish. He has a hundred pages so far, but the chapter titles alone tantalize me: "The Road to Kugitang," "About the Pomegranate with Rosy Petals," "Something Unknown about Pomegranates," "Dark Clouds on the Borderline," "The Holy Place of Shevlan."

Curiosity led me to the Kopet Dag Mountains in search of the original pomegranate forests and the man whose voice I was strangely drawn to. I was devastated to travel so far only to miss them both. But I've come to accept that the pomegranate has an unusual power over me. As red amphora-shaped blossoms sway on bare trees in the last days of autumn, I still imagine Persephone returning for her rendezvous in Hades' Underworld, while I am equally, and inexorably, drawn to this pomegranate specialist, Grigory Levin, and to a rural outpost in Turkmenistan called Garrygala.

DEBORAH SLICER

# APRICOT

A summer Taos sunset in your hand.
The weight of a small child's fist,
a girl, resisting sleep
as she sleeps.
The shape of a chicken angel's egg.
Eros's lovely clefted backside
in velvet. Fleshy
as a horse's lazy, lower lip.
A faraway fragrance:
juniper in gin, that slow gin
kiss.
What God saw on the eighth day, and ate, and said of it—
*way good.*
The woody stone we worry-gnaw when death's near,
when we're toothless again as babies,
trying to keep a great thought
small.

ALLISON WALLACE

# THE HONEYBEE'S METAPHOR

IN THE SWEET SECRECY of lavender twilight, hundreds of hexagonal wax cells hang suspended from light slats of pine. The back wall of every cell facing in one direction serves, Janus-like, as the back wall of another facing the opposite way; all of their open ends tip upward ever so slightly, cupping precious freight. Redolent of anther, pistil, petal, and nectar, each cell came painstakingly into being when fairy tongues and feet molded thousands of tiny wax flakes as they emerged from the upper abdomens of gold and black honeybees. Down low in the hive, the cells shelter plugs of white larvae on which the colony's near future rides; to the sides and just above, a rainbow of cells arches up and over, pixels of pollen grains, a protein-rich store neatly within reach of the nurse bees that use it to tend the fattening brood. And arching over and above still higher—in so high and wide a band as to require at least one, perhaps two additional stories or "supers" of wooden frames, hanging like office files in a cabinet—countless more of these tipped-up cells safeguard the shining wet labor of the late-spring field bees: clear tinctures of basswood, apple, cherry, pear, plum, and dandelion. Across, over, under, and about all these hundreds of cells, day and night, night into day, flow streams of honeybees—swollen rivers, whole watersheds of bees—constantly, tirelessly, at varying paces and in all directions. Yet they move not the least bit aimlessly. Born into a life of work, these infertile females—for that is what most of them are—live to do it well, to work so well at even the menial tasks assigned to them when young (like cleaning debris out of the hive) that they soon get promoted to the next job of importance (fanning their wings to cool things off, say), and still the next one (guarding the hive entrance, tending their queen), till finally they practice flight, they practice orienteering, they take to the air, to the fields, in search of water and pollen and sweet scents on the wind, in search of the summer-wide world. In search, finally, of nectar, from which every schoolchild knows they and their sisters will make honey.

Yellow, gold, amber. Sometimes a radiant burnt sienna. Tupelo, orange-blossom, raspberry, buckwheat, all-purpose wildflower. Rows of jars in the supermarkets, jars and plastic tubs and squeezable bears at every country roadside stand. Ubiquitous and familiar as honey has become, we forget that, for eons, men have scaled tree and cliff in its pursuit, sometimes falling in eager mid-reach to their deaths. That's desire for you: an irresistible if dangerous invitation, a compulsion not easily shaken off, an endless low-grade fever. But now, how tame it all seems. Now, after a little honey on our morning toast and a passing glance at the bee fumbling about a stem of clover, we moderns move on, unconcerned that honey—so readily had, no longer consciously an object of our desire—must nevertheless originate in desire. Not only that of the marketplace, which calls into being commercial production, but, more importantly, that of the bees themselves. But for *their* desire, honey would not happen. It is the one authentic answer to the honeybees' unfathomable, unstoppable urge for a taste of the world, for great bellyfuls of summer.

But what is the stuff, anyway, this honey? A naturally manufactured combination of simple sugars, some water, a few enzymes, vitamins, and minerals like potassium and magnesium. Minute quantities of pigments, along with aroma- and flavor-creating substances—the distilled essences of stem, leaf, petal, soil, and rain. Not to mention a little dose of whatever these things come burdened with, such as Imidan or Malathion. And honey also includes trace acids put there by the bees themselves, since the honey we ingest has already—quite necessarily, mind you, else nectar would never become honey—been partially digested by the stomach and salivary juices of all those hardworking, hard-flower-sucking, endlessly regurgitating bees. What is honey? Bee spit, you could say, so sometimes I do.

Or call it a more powerful sweetener, by about 25 percent, than sugar cane. Handy for making mead and hot toddies, for dressing wounds, for preserving bread or cookies or dead pharaohs. One of only two foods created by nature to be food and only food. Can you guess the other? Mammalian milk, all hands wave. Unlike seed, root, stalk, blossom, leaf, fruit, and flesh, milk and honey appear to exist for no earthly reason other than to feed young and to feed them richly, which may explain the conjuring power of that oft-repeated phrase. Honey is one of those subtle means by which, in Henry Thoreau's words, nature occasionally steals up into our veins, seducing us unawares with mineral, nutrient, water, and sugar—lacing the modern's otherwise jaded blood with desire after all, desire for the world's elemental constituents, a desire we didn't know we still had, such welcome if generally unacknowledged addiction.

Its sole purpose in life, so to speak, to be *food*, honey comes fully into its own only upon being eaten. Until then— in the hive, on the spoon—honey accomplishes no more than metaphor, no more than a figuring forth of ideas somewhat beside or beyond itself. It is ripeness, autumnal harvest, the growing season's promissory note paid in full. It is gold liquidated, a cup running over. The voluptuous ease of a morning spent in one's dressing gown, honey-as-metaphor is the antithesis of its workaholic makers. Honey is the lover whom you call by its mellifluous name. It is sunshine harnessed, summer resuscitated in a dark time, sweetness and light enthralled by viscous molecular chains.

But on the tongue, in the veins, honey becomes fantastically literal, the stuff not of figuration but rather transfiguration. Like any edible, honey transfigures and transforms because it is itself transformed, or rather *un*formed.

Suppose we set the honey pot aside for a moment to dwell on the larger, albeit ordinary, idea of food taken unto and into oneself, on the very idea of eating:

A strange business, ontologically speaking, is the act itself: one living form renders another form formless by tearing, chewing, and swallowing. Why should organic beings need literally to make their livings on the deaths and subsequent transformations of other beings? Whence and wherefore this all-important, life-defining function called metabolism, carried on constantly and by all manner of microbes, fish, fowl, fur-bearing fauna, toddlers, teenagers, even tenured university professors? To what end all these radical transgressions of intimate boundaries, these delicious violations? The biological "how" of eating is fairly well understood: in simple outline, eating means the appropriation, to my own body's use, of countless organic cells and, within these, an even greater horde of minerals, vitamins, nutrients, and energy "packets" called ATP molecules—matter and its inherent *potential* that recently worked in the service of an entirely other creature's existence, but that now serves my own. I secure my own immediate future by co-opting, in the most literal fashion imaginable, the would-be future of, say, a juicy summer tomato. And not long after I've eaten my fill, used billions of these ATP molecules and stashed away a few billion others, certain signals will flash from stomach to brain and I'll come back begging for more.

So much for the basic how of eating. The mystery of why remains with us. Ponder the insanity of a creator who would come up with a great, elaborate, incomparably beautiful creation that runs aright only when all its organic parts maintain their lives by destroying and eating each other. The sum-total of any amount of life on hand in the world at a given moment is also, when you think about it, a reasonable measure of the amount of death—death by disfiguration and digestion—occurring in the same moment. There really isn't even any in-between state (excepting maybe that of creatures frozen by glaciers or cryogenics): nature leaves nothing and no one simply lying about, without eating or being eaten, for long. Let malnutrition, weakness, and death overtake you, and something or other out there sharpens its tableware and falls to, with gusto. It has to, while seeing to its own interests. Of course, some of the diners in question aren't "out there" at all—they're *in* there: the aerobic bacteria in the gut of a fresh corpse soon use up the last of the available oxygen, then go anaerobic and fall to grazing on everything else from the inside out. Sure as you're born, it's eat or be eaten, digest or be digested. We're talking ordinary nature here, nature at its *most* ordinary, violent and violating, every bit as red in tooth and nail as it ever was, old as time but still hungry as hell. This is my mother, this—this "nature"—my mother, yes, but her nurturing love quickly turns devouring. My would-be murderess, she lies waiting, waiting for me to get sloppy and let down my guard.

And so I sup. I eat to perpetuate my very self, to propel myself into the future that awaits, I trust, my whole and healthy arrival. As a child I ate just to *become* myself. Like all of you, I was born fortunate, into the smart, opportunistic line of *Homo sapiens*, with lots of edibles to choose from: lots of other living forms I could happily dismember, dismantle, disfigure, and digest, everything from parsley to parsnips, chickens to chickpeas, selves of a sort that had in their turn tried overtaking the future by dining as heartily as nature and luck would allow. We have all of us eaten to live, to grow, to work and play—to satisfy, says Leon Kass in *The Hungry Soul*, the physical prerequisites of ambition, the desire to do more than eat. But also true is that we have lived to eat again. We still do, we're doing it now, metabolizing without effort, living for the next chance to insist on union with some Other—to insist with all due vehemence on *more of the world*. Has it occurred to you that your life in this world is sometimes a lonely business? Indeed: try going without a bite of it for a long while, then just see if you can find another kind of loneliness more horrific, more intolerable.

Give us more of the summer-wide world, murmur the honeybees, and still more, as September eases toward October, toward All Hallows Eve. Theirs is a less bloody means of achieving "more" than ours, since they deal far less in integral, ontologically complete or recognizable forms: liquid nectar merely borrows its shape temporarily from the flower that cups it. In like manner honey owes its principal form to whatever contains it—wax cell, Mason jar, large intestine. So

relatively formless is extracted honey that its consumption—
whether by a bee or a woman—seems a fairly gentle act,
according happily with the conceit that this is honey's finest
hour, its rendezvous with destiny.

More, say the honeybees, and still more. But every
autumn there comes a day when there is no more, when no
nectar flows, when desire meets only with disappointment.
The days darken, the fall blooms of aster and goldenrod
shrivel and drop, the fields frost over. At such a crisis the
bees cannot make do with parsnips or chicken, so the honey
they have stored becomes everything to them. Should the
supply fail before the nectar flows again, the colony will
starve. It's an edible land we share with the bees and the rest
of creation, but selectively so: no one thing can get by on just
anything (though the common cockroach comes close). If all
of creation is destined to hunger for some other part or parts
of creation, then so are all but the very richest of us doomed
to know, on occasion, those fabled pangs of deprivation—the
stabbing regret of the hook that comes up clean, the spear
that falls short, the wallet that gapes open like a mouth. Pairs
of twin dervishes—desire and disappointment, consumma-
tion and content—spin round and through us all, trailing
scarves of soil and water, wind and sunlight, binding we the
living and the dying to each other, keeping all the organic
world in exquisitely painful need and search of intimate
relationship to itself. Like sex, like prayer, eating is an urge
toward union (which may suggest why sex and religion so often use its language, its imagery). Eating is sweet fulfillment,
disaster deferred once again, the gift of a few more hours in
which to think about something else, however unimportant
or superfluous it may be to this one, all-embracing mandate.
Time to think about summer, perhaps, the honey-gold glow
of a beer sipped on a back porch. About the tomatoes that

are almost ready for picking and canning. About those bees over there, a dozen or more of them in the clover, fondling petals and pollen.

ROBIN MACARTHUR

# SUGARING

HALF THE PEOPLE on your road park their cars near the
highway and walk; the other half fasten their seatbelts, take a
deep breath, and gun it, bucking ruts and jerking wheels as
their bodies get slammed this way and that. The kids on the
school bus hold on to the seats in front of them and scream
as the bus driver (your mother) presses the pedal to the floor,
tightens her jaw, and keeps the bus pointed forward with bed-
rock determination. Car struts get shot, the alignment goes
out of whack. You step out of your car in the driveway and
your boots sink down six inches. You track it onto the porch,
and into the hall, and into the kitchen. Ten miles away, in the
town with paved streets, people are wearing sundresses and
sandals; you're still in jeans and the Muck Boots you've been
wearing for six months straight. Around here, March and
April are called "mud season."

But there is one consolation. Mud season is also sugaring
season. They go hand in hand during these cold nights, warm
days. The frost under the roads settles, creating sinkholes; the
sap in the maple trees runs, filling buckets. You walk down
the road with your two-year-old daughter to the sugarhouse,

looking, hoping, for steam, and there it is: a thick waft of sweet, moist air billowing out of the vented roof. Inside, your parents are throwing logs into the evaporator, checking levels, pouring beautiful resin-colored syrup into the glass Mason jars neighbors have brought by. Firelight shimmers through the cracks of the iron doors. You run across the (muddy) road with your daughter to collect sap and watch her press her lips against the metal spigot; from where you stand it looks like she is kissing the tree. "Yum!" she exclaims, pulling away, her face smeared with sap and tree bark and moss and snot.

People drop by: a family bearing bowls of soup, a single man proffering a six-pack of beer. It's an open house, the sugar shack, and everyone knows it. This dropping in is a way of keeping the sugar makers company—they're in here for ten hours at a time most days—but it's also what happens to people in spring. You begin to thaw. You want to see faces again, converse, be outside for long stretches of time. Neighbors bring in wood; you scoop scum from the back pans; your daughter pulls out empty plastic jugs for your mother to fill. The fire hisses. The steam rises. You crack open beers. A party: "Sugar Boogie," your dad and daughter call it.

That night you make pizzas, cooking them on the open grate of the evaporator door. You throw on red pepper, fresh mozzarella, pesto from last summer's garden. You sit on old tractor and bus seats turned into makeshift chairs and eat off your hands. Later someone steps through the door with a bottle of Glenlivet and cups. Last year you all determined, after much sampling, the perfect combination of scotch and near-syrup; now you attempt to find that perfect ratio once more. Outside it grows dark. The room fills with hooting laughter. Once in a while you hear a car revving up the road, gunning it through deep pockets of mud. You watch the steam, the fire, the glistening faces, and you're glad you're not in that car, out on those roads, trying to get somewhere.

You step out the back door to take a leak in the snow and look up—sparks shooting out of the rusted chimney, an ash-flecked moon rising above the trees. You could go back inside, but instead you linger for a while: pants down, grinning, grateful for this dissolution of walls and of boundaries between inside and out, for this synchronicity between what the trees do and what people do, for the fact that it's (finally) warm enough for you to be out here half-naked, knee deep in a pile of snow, not wanting to be anywhere but the very spot your boots are planted.

# CONTRIBUTORS

**Tamar Adler** has worked as a chef, magazine editor, and cooking teacher. The author of *An Everlasting Meal: Cooking with Economy and Grace*, she lives in Brooklyn, New York.

**Barbara L. Baer** is the author of the novella *Grisha the Scrivener*. She lives in Sonoma County, California, where she cultivates an organic orchard and garden.

**Tamara Dean** is the author of *The Human-Powered Home: Choosing Muscles over Motors* and several college textbooks. Her stories and essays have appeared in *The American Scholar*, *Bellevue Literary Review*, *Creative Nonfiction*, *New Ohio Review*, and elsewhere. She also produces radio features and cofounded the community radio station WDRT in Viroqua, Wisconsin.

**Jane Hirshfield** is the author of seven books of poetry, most recently *Come, Thief* and *After*; four books collecting and cotranslating the work of poets from the past; and a volume of essays. A current Chancellor of the Academy of American Poets, her other honors include fellowships from the Guggenheim and Rockefeller foundations and the National Endowment for the Arts. Her work appears in *The New Yorker*, *The Atlantic*, *Poetry*, and seven editions of *The Best American Poetry*. A new book of poems and a new book of essays are forthcoming in 2015.

**Barbara Kingsolver**'s fourteen books of fiction, poetry, and creative nonfiction include the novels *The Bean Trees*, *The Poisonwood Bible*, and *The Lacuna*. Translated into more than twenty languages, her work has won a devoted worldwide readership, a place in the core English literature curriculum, and many awards, including the National Humanities Medal. Her fiction has been three times shortlisted and one time a winner of Britain's Orange Prize.

**Maxine Kumin**'s eighteenth book of poetry, *And Short the Season*, was published in April 2014 by W.W. Norton. *Publishers Weekly* named it one of the spring's top ten poetry titles. Her seventeenth collection, *Where I Live: New and Selected Poems 1990–2010*, won the Los Angeles Times Book Prize in 2011. She was a Robert Frost and Harvard University arts medalist. A U.S. poet laureate and Pulitzer Prize winner, she lived with her husband on a farm in New Hampshire until her death in February 2014.

**Laurie Kutchins** has published three books of poetry, including *The Night Path*, which received the Isabella Gardener Award and was nominated for a Pulitzer Prize. Her poems and essays have appeared widely in *Orion, Ploughshares, The New Yorker, The Georgia Review, LIT, The Southern Review*, and other places. She teaches at James Madison University, and divides her time between the Shenandoah Valley and Teton Valley.

**Robin MacArthur** is a writer, educator, and one-half of the musical duo Red Heart the Ticker. She lives with her husband and two young children in a self-built house on the land where she was born in Marlboro, Vermont. Her essays and stories have appeared in *Hunger Mountain, Orion, Whole*

*Terrain, Shenandoah, Alaska Quarterly,* and on NPR. When not writing, singing, teaching, or house-building, she spends her time helping out on her mother's organic farm and traipsing through woods with her children, Avah Margaret and Owen Cricket.

**Gary Paul Nabhan** is the W. K. Kellogg endowed chair in sustainable food systems at the Southwest Center of the University of Arizona. He is also an orchard keeper, seed saver, and agro-ecologist. His work with food and localization dates back to the 1970s, and his book, *Coming Home to Eat,* along with Joan Gussie's *This Organic Life,* is considered among the early manifestos of the local food movement. His latest book, *Cumin, Camels, and Caravans: A Spice Odyssey,* is available from University of California Press.

**Aimee Nezhukumatathil** is the author of three award-winning collections of poetry: *Lucky Fish, At the Drive-In Volcano,* and *Miracle Fruit.* Her honors include the Pushcart Prize and a poetry fellowship from the National Endowment for the Arts. She is Professor of English at SUNY-Fredonia, where she received a Chancellor's Medal of Excellence. She lives in western New York with her husband and their two young sons.

**Joni Tevis** is the author of a book of lyric essays, *The Wet Collection,* published by Milkweed Editions. She teaches literature and creative writing at Furman University in Greenville, South Carolina, and is finishing a new book of nonfiction about ghost towns, tourist traps, and atomic dread. It is forthcoming from Milkweed Editions.

**Deborah Slicer** is a philosophy professor and directs the masters program in environmental philosophy at the University of Montana. Her collection of poetry, *The White Calf Kicks*, won the 2003 Autumn House Prize, which was judged by Naomi Shihab Nye.

**Katrina Vandenberg** is the author of two books of poetry, *The Alphabet Not Unlike the World* and *Atlas*. She teaches in the Creative Writing Programs at Hamline University, and serves as poetry editor for *Water~Stone Review*.

**Allison Wallace** was born near New Orleans and educated at the Universities of Mississippi–Oxford and North Carolina–Chapel Hill. She is now associate professor of American studies in the Honors College at the University of Central Arkansas. She is passionate about nature, wherever it is found: on farms and ranches, in suburban backyards, in wilderness and city greenspace, even in our meals. Reading, teaching, beekeeping, gardening, hiking, and canoeing fill her time and keep her sane.

# ABOUT ORION MAGAZINE

SINCE 1982, *Orion* has been a meeting place for people who seek a conversation about nature and culture that is rooted in beauty, imagination, and hope. Through the written word, the visual arts, and the ideas of our culture's most imaginative thinkers, *Orion* seeks to craft a vision for a better future for both people and planet.

Reader-supported and totally advertising-free, *Orion* blends scientific thinking with the arts, and the intellectual with the emotional. *Orion* has a long history of publishing the work of established writers from Wendell Berry, Terry Tempest Williams, and Barry Lopez to Rebecca Solnit, Luis Alberto Urrea, and Sandra Steingraber.

*Orion* is also grounded in the visual arts, publishing picture essays and art portfolios that challenge the traditional definition of "environment" and invite readers to think deeply about their place in the natural world. *Orion*'s website, www.orionmagazine.org, features multimedia web extras including slide shows and author interviews, as well as opportunities for readers to discuss *Orion* articles.

*Orion* is published bimonthly by The Orion Society, a nonprofit 501(c)3 organization, and is available in both print and digital editions.

## Subscribe

*Orion* publishes six beautiful, inspiring issues per year. To get a free trial issue, purchase a subscription, or order a gift subscription, please visit www.orionmagazine.org/subscribe or call 888/254-3713.

## Support

*Orion* depends entirely on the generous support of readers and foundations to publish the magazine and books like this one. To support *Orion*, please visit www.orionmagazine.org/donate, or send a contribution directly to *Orion* at 187 Main Street, Great Barrington, MA, 01230.

   To discuss making a gift of stock or securities, or for information about how to include *Orion* in your estate plans, please call us at 888/909-6568, or send an e-mail to development@orionmagazine.org.

## Shop

Head to the *Orion* website, www.orionmagazine.org, to purchase *Orion* books, organic cotton t-shirts, and other merchandise featuring the distinctive *Orion* logo. Back issues from the past thirty years are also available.

# MORE BOOKS FROM ORION

## ORION READERS

Orion Readers collect landmark *Orion* essays into short thematic volumes:

*Change Everything Now.* A selection of essays about ecological urgency.

*Thirty-Year Plan: Thirty Writers on What We Need to Build a Better Future.* An eloquent statement on the future of humanity.

*Wonder and Other Survival Skills.* A collection of thoughtful and inspirational writing on our relationship to the natural world.

*Leave No Child Inside.* Essays that propose a radical reconnection of children and nature through education.

*Animals & People.* A selection of essays that celebrate our connection to the animal world, with a foreword by Jane Goodall.

*Beyond Ecophobia: Reclaiming the Heart in Nature Education,* by David Sobel. An expanded version of one of *Orion*'s most popular articles that speaks to those interested in nurturing in children the ability to understand and care deeply for nature from an early age.

*Into the Field: A Guide to Locally Focused Learning,* by Claire Walker Leslie, John Tallmadge, and Tom Wessels, with an introduction by Ann Zwinger. Curriculum ideas for teachers interested in taking their students out of doors.

*Place-Based Education: Connecting Classrooms & Communities,* by David Sobel. A guide for using the local community and environment as the starting place for curriculum learning, strengthening community bonds, appreciation for the natural world, and a commitment to citizen engagement.

## ORION ANTHOLOGIES

*Finding Home: Writing on Nature and Culture from* Orion *Magazine,* edited by Peter Sauer. An anthology of the best writing from *Orion* published from 1982 to 1992.

*The Future of Nature: Writing on a Human Ecology from* Orion *Magazine,* selected and introduced by Barry Lopez. An anthology of the best writing from *Orion* published from 1992 to 2007.

## FOR EDUCATORS

Ideal for reading groups and academic course adoption, many *Orion* books are accompanied by a downloadable teacher's guide consisting of key discussion questions. Teacher's guides can be found on the *Orion* website at www.orionmagazine .org/education.

Series design by Hans Teensma,
principal of the design studio Impress
(www.impressinc.com), which has
designed *Orion* since 1998.
The typeface is Scala, designed by Dutch
typographer Martin Majoor in 1990.
Printed by BookMobile.